QUICK & EASY

Italian

learn the basics with the easy-to-follow CD and book

QUICK & EASY italian

City guide compiled by Rob Alcraft
Translations by The ASK Group Ltd
Map by Hardlines

Published by Top That! Publishing plc
Tide Mill Way, Woodbridge, Suffolk, IPI2 IAP, UK
www.topthatpublishing.com
Copyright © 2011 Top That! Publishing plc
2 4 6 8 9 7 5 3
Printed and bound in China

CONTENTS

QUICK AND EASY ITALIAN

Visiting a new country is always exciting, but basic language barriers can be a problem. Designed to give you a command of basic phrases, this Quick and Easy language guide will make communicating in another language simple, enabling you to ask for what you need in everyday situations and understand other people's responses.

Each English phrase is given with its Italian equivalent, and a guide to pronunciation. The guide is arranged in easy reference sections, and you can use it as an on-the-spot reminder. Accompanying the book is a CD containing 200 essential phrases so that you can learn some of the basics before gaining confidence in your pronunciation.

With the worries of communication out of the way you can be free to enjoy your stay. To help make the most of it you can use the handy city guide at the back of this book which includes tips on getting around Rome and the best attractions that shouldn't be missed.

PRONUNCIATION GUIDE

If you have difficulty pronouncing any of the Italian words, simply look up the sound you are having difficulty with in this table. Alongside each Italian sound there is an English word containing a similar sound. Alternatively use the CD and learn the phases marked with the CD symbol.

ITALIAN SOUND	LETTERS USED IN TRANSLITERATION	PRONOUNCED AS IN ENGLISH WORD
au	ow	out
c (except when followed by i or e)	k or c	cup
c (followed by i or e)	ch	chair
ch	k or c	cup
er	air	air
g (expect when followed by i or e)	g	good
g (followed by i or e)	j	juice
gh	g	good
gli	lyee	–
gn	ny	onion
gui	gwee	Gwynedd
o	o	pot
sc	sh	shop
sch	sk	mask
z	ts	paints

Note: the letter 'r' should always be slightly rolled.

EVERYDAY ITALIAN

BASIC PHRASES

	English	Italian	Pronunciation
😊	Yes	Sì	See
😊	No	No	No
😊	Thank you	Grazie	Gratseeay
	Ok	OK/d'accordo	Daakordo
😊	Good, great	Bene, ottimo	Baynay/ot-timo
😊	That's fine	Perfetto	Pairfaytto
	That's right	Giusto	Joosto
	Hi	Ciao	Chow
😊	Hello	Salve	Saalvay
😊	Goodbye	Arrivederci	Arreevaydairche
😊	Good morning	Buongiorno	Bwon jorno
😊	Good afternoon	Buona sera /Buon pomeriggio	Bwona saira /Bwon pomaireejo
😊	Goodnight	Buona notte	Bwona nottay
😊	I don't understand.	Non capisco.	Non kaapeesko
😊	What does this mean?	Cosa significa?	Koza seenyeefica?
	See you later.	A più tardi.	A peew tardee.
😊	Pleased to meet you.	Piacere di conoscerla.	Peea-chairay dee konoshairla.
😊	How are you?	Come sta?	Komay sta?
😊	I'm very well, thanks.	Molto bene, grazie.	Molto baynay, gratseeay.
	What's your name?	Come si chiama?	Komay see keeama?
	This is my husband.	Questo è mio marito.	Kwaysto eh meeo mareeto.
	This is my wife.	Questa è mia moglie.	Kwaysta eh meea mo-lyay.
	This is my son.	Questo è mio figlio.	Kwaysto eh meeo fee-lyo.
	This is my daughter.	Questa è mia figlia.	Kwaysta eh meea fee-lya.
	This is my colleague.	Questo è un mio collega (M). /questa è una mia collega (F).	Kwaysto eh oon meeo kollayga. /kwaysta eh oona meea kollayga.
😊	Excuse me	Mi scusi	Mee skoozee
😊	Do you speak English?	Parla inglese?	Parla eenglayzay?
	Could you say that again?	Può ripetere, per favore?	Pwo reepaytairay, pair fa-voray?
😊	Can you speak more slowly, please?	Parli più lentamente, per favore?	Parlee peew layntamayntay, pair fa-voray?
	Please can you write it down for me?	Può scriverlo, per favore?	Pwo skreevairlo, pair fa-voray?
	Can you help me please?	Mi può aiutare, per favore?	Mee pwo ah-u-taray pair fa-voray?

😊 = Phrase featured on CD

ABOUT YOU

My name is...	Mi chiamo...	Mee keeamo
I'm married/not married.	Sono sposato (M)/sposata (F) /non sono sposato (M)/ sposata (F).	Sono spozaato /spozaata /non sono spozaato/ spozaata.
I have... children.	Ho... figli.	Oh... fee-lyee.
I live in...	Vivo a...	Veevo ah...
I'm staying at...	Alloggio a...	Allojo ah...
I'm on holiday.	Sono in vacanza.	Sono een vacaantsaa.
I'm here on business.	Sono qui per lavoro.	Sono kwee pair lavoro.
I'm here for... days/weeks.	Resto qui per... giorni/ settimane.	Raysto kwee pair... jornee/ saytteemanay.
I've come from...	Arrivo da...	Areevo da...
I'm going to...	Sto andando a...	Sto andaando ah...

HEARING

Can I help you?	Posso aiutarla?	Posso ahutaarla?
What do you want?	Coza desidera?	Koza dezeedaira?
What are you looking for?	Cosa sta cercando?	Koza sta chairkando?
What is your name?	Come si chiama?	Komay see keeama?
Have you booked?	Ha prenotato?	Ah prenotaato?

BASIC REQUESTS

I WANT...

I want...	Vorrei...	Vor-ray...
/a room.	/una stanza.	/oona stantsa.
/something to drink.	/qualcosa da bere.	/kwalkoza da bairay.
/something to eat.	/qualcosa da mangiare.	/kwalkoza da man-jaray.

WHAT?

English	Italian	Pronunciation
What is the time?	Che ora è?	Kay ora eh?
What is your name?	Come si chiama?	Komay see keeama?
What is the problem?	Qual è il problema?	Kwal eh eel problayma?

WHERE?

Where is...	Dove è...	Dov eh...
/the bank?	/la banca?	la banka?
/the park?	/il parco?	eel paarko?

WHEN?

When...	Quando...	Kwando...
/does the film start?	/comincia il film?	/komeencha eel film?
/does the gallery open?	/apre la galleria?	/apray la gallay-reea?

HOW?

How much is it?	Quanto costa?	Kwanto kosta?
How do I get there?	Come ci arrivo?	komay chee arreevo?

CONTRASTS

It is...	È...	Eh...
good/bad	buono/cattivo	bwono/katteevo
big/small	grande/piccolo	graanday/peekolo
high/low	alto/basso	alto/basso
expensive/cheap	costoso/economico	kostozo/ekonomiko
busy/empty	occupato/vuoto	okkoopato/vwoto
old/new	vecchio/nuovo	vaykeeo/nwovo
fast/slow	veloce/lento	vaylochay/laynto
quiet/noisy	silenzioso/rumoroso	seelayntseeozo/roomorozo
hot/cold	caldo/freddo	kaaldo/frayddo
open/shut	aperto/chiuso	apairto/keeoozo
interesting/boring	interessante/noioso	eenteray-santay/noeeozo
I like it.	Mi piace.	Mee peea-chay.
I don't like it.	Non mi piace.	Non mee peea-chay.

NUMBERS

English	Italian	Pronunciation
one	uno	oono
two	due	dooay
three	tre	tray
four	quattro	kwattro
five	cinque	cheenkway
six	sei	sayee
seven	sette	settay
eight	otto	otto
nine	nove	novay
ten	dieci	dee-aychee
eleven	undici	oondeechee
twelve	dodici	dodeechee
thirteen	tredici	traydeechee
fourteen	quattordici	kwattordeechee
fifteen	quindici	kweendeechee
sixteen	sedici	saydeechee
seventeen	diciassette	deecheeassayttay
eighteen	diciotto	deechotto
nineteen	diciannove	deechannovay
twenty	venti	vayntee
twenty-one	ventuno	vayntoono
twenty-two	ventidue	vaynteedooay
thirty	trenta	traynta
thirty-one	trentuno	trayntoono
thirty-two	trentadue	trayntadooay
forty	quaranta	kwaranta
fifty	cinquanta	cheenkwanta
sixty	sessanta	sayssanta
seventy	settanta	sayttanta
eighty	ottanta	ottanta
ninety	novanta	novanta
one hundred	cento	chaynto
one hundred and ten	centodieci	chaynto-deeaychee
one hundred and twenty	centoventi	chaynto-vayntee
five hundred	cinquecento	cheenkway-chaynto
one thousand	mille	meellay
five thousand	cinquemila	cheenkwaymeela
one million	un milione	oon meeleeone

TIME, DATES AND SEASONS

TIME

today	**oggi**	ojee
tonight	**stanotte**	stanottay
this morning	**stamattina**	sta matteena
tomorrow morning	**domattina**	domatteena
afternoon	**pomeriggio**	pomaireejo
tomorrow afternoon	**domani**	daw-mani
	pomeriggio	pomaireejo
this evening	**stasera**	stasaira
tomorrow evening	**domani**	daw-mani
	sera	saira
midday	**mezzogiorno**	maytso jorno
midnight	**mezzanotte**	maytsanottay
yesterday	**ieri**	eeairee
this week	**questa**	kwaysta
	settimana	saytteemana
next week	**la prossima**	la prossima
	settimana	saytteemana
later on	**più tardi**	peew tardee
hour	**ora**	ora
half past	**...e mezza**	ay maytsa
quarter past	**...e un quarto**	ay oon kwarto
quarter to	**...meno un quarto**	mayno oon kwarto
four o'clock	**le quattro**	lay kwattro
ten past four	**le quattro e dieci**	lay kwattro ay deeaychee
half past four	**le quattro e mezza**	lay kwattro ay maytsa
quarter to five	**le cinque meno un quarto**	lay cheenkway mayno oon kwarto

DATES AND SEASONS

1st March	**Primo marzo**	Preemo martso
23rd March	**Ventitré marzo**	Vaynteetray martso
January	**Gennaio**	Jaynnaaeeo
February	**Febbraio**	Faybbraaeeo
March	**Marzo**	Martso
April	**Aprile**	Apreelay
May	**Maggio**	Majo
June	**Giugno**	Joonyo
July	**Luglio**	Loo-lyo
August	**Agosto**	Agosto
September	**Settembre**	Settembray
October	**Ottobre**	Ottobray
November	**Novembre**	Novembray
December	**Dicembre**	Deechembray
Spring	**Primavera**	Preemavaira
Summer	**Estate**	Aystatay
Autumn	**Autunno**	Owtoonno
Winter	**Inverno**	Eenvairno

MONEY

Where is the nearest bank?	Dov'è la banca più vicina?	Doveh la banka peew veecheena?
When does the bank open?	Quando apre la banca?	Kwando apray la banka?
Is there a cash point near here?	C'è un bancomat nei dintorni?	Chay oon bankomat nay deentorni?
Where can I cash these traveller's cheques?	Dove posso cambiare questi traveller's cheques?	Dovay posso kambeearay kwaystee travellers cheques?
What is the exchange rate?	Qual'è il tasso di cambio?	Kwaleh eel tasso dee kambeeo?
Could I have some smaller notes please?	Posso avere banconote di taglio più piccolo, per favore?	Posso avairay banko-notay dee ta-lyo peew peekolo, pair fa-voray?
Could I have some coins please?	Posso avere delle monete, per favore?	Posso avairay dayllay monaytay, pair fa-voray?

HEARING

Can I see...	Per favore, mi fa vedere...	Pair fa-voray, mee fa vedairay...
/some identification?	/un documento?	/oon dokoomaynto?
/your passport?	/il passaporto?	/eel passaporto?
/your card?	/la carta d'identità?	/la karta dee-dayntee-ta?
How much do you want?	Quanto vuole?	Kwanto vwolay?
Please sign here.	Firmi qui, per favore.	Feermee kwee, pair fa-voray.
What's your address in Italy?	Qual'è il suo indirizzo in Italia?	Kwaleh eel swo eendeereetso een eetaleea?

PROBLEMS

The machine has eaten my card.	Il bancomat non mi ha restituito la carta.	Eel bankomat non mee ah raysteetweeto la karta
My card won't work.	La mia carta non funziona.	La meea karta non foontseeona
Could I check my balance?	Posso controllare il mio saldo?	Posso kontro-laaray eel meeo saldo?
Can you call my bank?	Può chiamare la mia banca?	Pwo keeamaaray la meea banka?
Please will you check with my bank.	Controlli con la mia banca, per favore.	Kontrollee kon la meea banka pair fa-voray.

POST

USEFUL WORDS

all transactions	**tutte le operazioni**	toottay lay opairatseeonee
bank	**banca**	banka
buy	**comprare**	kom-praray
cash desk	**cassa**	kassa
cash machine /ATM	**bancomat**	bankomat
cashier	**cassiere**	kasseeairay
charge	**spese**	spayzay
closed	**chiuso**	keeoozo
commission	**commissione**	kommeesseeonay
credit card	**carta di credito**	karta dee kraydito
deposit	**deposito**	daypozeeto
identification	**documento d'identità**	dokoomaynto dee-daynty-ta
exchange rate	**tasso di cambio**	tasso dee kambeeo
from	**da**	da
money	**denaro**	daynaro
notes	**banconote**	banko-notay
open	**aperto**	apairto
pounds sterling	**sterlina**	stairleena
withdrawal	**prelievo**	prayleeayvo

Can I have stamps for letters to the UK please? **Vorrei dei francobolli per lettera per il Regno Unito, per favore** Vo-ray day francobollee pair lettaira pair eel raynyo ooneeto, pair fa-voray

- Where can I post this? **Dove posso imbucarla?** Dovay posso eembookarla?
- Where can I buy stamps? **Dove posso comprare dei francobolli?** Dovay posso kom-praray day frankobollee?

- Do you sell... /postcards? /stamps? **Vendete... /cartoline? /francobolli?** Vendaytay... /karto-leenay? /frankobollee?

How much to send... /this letter? /this parcel? **Quanto costa spedire... /questa lettera? /questo pacco?** Kwanto kosta spaydeeray... /kwaysta lettaira /kwaysto pakko

- I want to send this to Ireland /the UK /the USA **Voglio spedirla in Irlanda /nel Regno Unito/negli Stati Uniti.** Vo-lyo spaydeerlo een eerlanda /nayl raynyo ooneeto/naylyee statee ooneeti/

HEARING

Where do you want to send this? **Dove vuole spedirla?** Dovay vwolay spaydeerla

Write the address here. **Scriva l'indirizzo qui.** Skreeva l'een-deereetso kwee.

TELEPHONES

Is there a public telephone here?	C'è un telefono pubblico qui?	Chay oon tay-lay-fono poobb-liko kwee?
May I use your telephone?	Posso usare il suo telefono?	Posso oozaray eel swo taylay-fono?
Where can I buy a phone card?	Dove posso comprare una scheda telefonica?	Dovay posso kom-praray oona skayda taylayfoneeka?
Do you have change for the telephone?	Ha delle monete per il telefono?	Ah dayllay monaytay pair eel taylay-fono?
What is the telephone number here?	Qual'è il numero di telefono di questo apparecchio?	Kwaleh eel noo-may-ro dee taylayfono dee kwaysto appahrekkeo?
What number do I call to get the operator?	Quale numero devo fare per parlare con l'operatore	Kwalay noo-may-ro dayvo faray pair parlaray kon lopairatoray?
/directory enquiries?	/con il servizio informazioni telefoniche?	/kon eel sairveetseeo eenformat-seeonee taylay-foneekay?

HEARING

Who's speaking?	Chi parla?	Kee parla?
They're not here.	Non ci sono.	Non chee sono
Can you call back?	Può richiamare?	Pwo rikeea-maaray?
Can I take a message?	Vuole lasciare un messaggio?	Vwolay lashiaaray oon mayssajo?
What's the number you want to call?	Qual'è il numero da chiamare?	Kwaleh eel noo-may-ro da keea-maray?
Can you repeat that?	Può ripetere, per favore?	Pwo reepaytairay pair fa-voray?

USEFUL WORDS

call box	cabina telefonica	kabeena taylayfonika
change	monete	monaytay
dial	digitare	deejeetaaray
engaged	occupato	okkoopato
form	modulo	mo-doolo
letter	lettera	lettaira
number	numero	noo-may-ro
operator	operatore	opairatoray
place	località	lokalee-ta
postcode	codice postale	kodeechay posta-lay

MAKING A CALL

English	Italian	Pronunciation
Can I speak to...?	Posso parlare con...?	Posso parlaaray kon...?
When will they be back?	Quando rientrano?	Kwando reeayntrano?
Can you ask them to call me, please?	Può dire loro di richiamarmi, per favore?	Pwo deera loro dee rikeea-maarmee, pair fa-voray?
I don't speak much Italian. Can you speak English?	Non parlo molto l'ital-iano. Lei parla inglese?	Non parlo molto leetaleeaano. Lay parla eenglayzay?
Can you say that again, please?	Può ripetere, per favore?	Pwo reepaytairay pair fa-voray?
Hold on a moment, please.	Attenda in linea, per favore.	Attaynda een leenaya pair fa-voray.
I will call later.	Chiamo più tardi.	Keeamo peew tardee.
Can I reverse the charges?	Posso chiamare a carico del destinatario?	Posso keea-maray ah kaarico del daysteenatareeo?

DIRECTIONS

Where is the nearest...?	Dov'è il... più vicino?	Doveh eel ... peew veecheeno?
How do I get to...?	Come arrivo a...?	Komay arreevo ah...?
Can you show me where we are on this map, please?	Può mostrarmi dove siamo su questa pianta, per favore?	Pwo mostraarmi dovay seeamo soo kwaysta peeanta, pair fa-voray?
I'm lost.	Mi sono perso.	Mee sono pairso
I need to get to...	Devo andare a...	Dayvo an-daaray ah...
Can you help me please?	Mi può aiutare, per favore?	Mee pwo ah-u-taaray pair fa-voray?

HEARING

You're going the wrong way.	Sta sbagliando strada.	Sta sba-lyando straada
Where are you going?	Dove sta andando?	Dovay sta andaando?
Keep going this way.	Continui su questa strada.	Konteenooee soo kwaysta straada.
Go that way.	Vada in quella direzione.	Vada een kwella deeretseeonay
Go left.	Vada a sinistra.	Vada ah seeneestra.
Go right.	Vada a destra.	Vada ah daystra.
Go straight on.	Vada dritto.	Vada dreetto.

There, you can see it.	Là, si vede da qui.	La, see vayday da kwee.
Over there.	Laggiù.	Lajoo
Over the road.	Oltre la strada.	Oltray la straada.
I don't know.	Non lo so.	Non lo so
Follow that sign.	Segua quel-l'indicazione.	Saygwa kwayll eendeekatseeonay

USEFUL WORDS

alley	vicolo	vikolo
bridge	ponte	pontay
building	edificio	edeefeecho
cathedral	cattedrale	kattay-dralay
door	porta	porta
entrance	entrata	ayn-trata
gate	cancello/gate	kanchayllo
hotel	hotel	ohtel
left	sinistra	seeneestra
lift	ascensore	ashayn-soray
museum	museo	moo-zayo
right	destra	daystra
shopping centre	centro commerciale	chayntro kommair-chalay
signposted	sul cartello stradale	sool kartayllo stra-dalay
square	piazza	peeatsa
straight	dritto	dreetto
street	strada	straada
tower	torre	torray
wall	muro	mooro

TRAVEL

HEARING

Where are you travelling to?	Dove vuole andare?	Dovay vwolay an-daray?
When do you want to leave? /travel?	Quando vuole partire? /andare?	Kwando vwolay parteeray? /an-daray?
How many people are travelling?	Quante persone siete?	Kwantay pair-sonay seeaytay?
There's no train /bus today.	Non ci sono treni /autobus oggi.	Non chee sono traynee /owtoboos ojee
It's leaving now.	Sta partendo ora.	Sta partayndo ora.

... ON THE BUS

Where can I catch the bus to...?	Dove posso prendere l'autobus per...?	Dovay posso prayndairay low-toboos pair...?
What number bus should I catch for...?	Quale autobus devo prendere per...?	Kwalay owto-boos dayvo prayndairay pair...?
☺ Do you know when the next bus is?	Sa quando c'è il prossimo autobus?	Sa kwando chay eel prossimo owtoboos?
☺ Can you tell me how often they run?	Può dirmi ogni quanto tempo passa?	Pwo deermee onyee kwanto taympo passa?

Can I buy a ticket on the bus?	Posso comprare il biglietto sull'autobus?	Posso kom-praray eel beel-yet-to sool owtoboos?
☺ How much is the fare to...?	Quanto costa arrivare a...?	Kwanto kosta arree-varay ah...?
☺ Does this bus go to...?	Questo autobus va a...?	Kwaysto owtoboos va ah?

... METRO AND TAXI

☺ Where is the nearest metro station?	Dov'è la stazione di metropolitana più vicina?	Doveh la statseeonay dee maytropoleetana peew veecheena?
☺ Where can I get a metro map?	Dove posso trovare una piantina della metropolitana?	Dovay posso tro-varay oona pee-anteena daylla maytropoleetana?
Where can I buy a metro ticket?	Dove posso comprare un biglietto per la metropolitana?	Dovay posso kom-praray oon beel-yet-to pair la maytropolee-tana?

Where can I get a taxi?	**Dove posso trovare un taxi?**	Dovay posso tro-varay oon taxi?
I want to go to…	**Vorrei andare a…**	Vo-ray an-daray ah…
How much will it cost to…?	**Quanto costa il biglietto fino a…?**	Kwanto kosta eel beel-yet-to feeno ah…?

… ON THE TRAIN

When is the next train for…?	**Quando parte il prossimo treno per…?**	Kwando partay eel prossimo trayno pair…?
How often is the train for…	**Ogni quanto tempo partono i treni per…**	Onyee kwanto taympo partono e traynee pair…?
Can I have a copy of the timetable?	**Posso avere una copia dell'orario dei treni?**	Posso avairay oona kopeea dayll orareeo day traynee?
Where can I buy a ticket for…?	**Dove posso comprare un biglietto per…?**	Dovay posso kom-praray oon beel-yet-to pair…?
Two tickets for…	**Due biglietti per…**	Dooay beel-yet-tee pair…
Two single tickets for…	**Due biglietti di sola andata per…**	Doo-ay beel-yet-tee dee solaa andata pair…
I'd like return tickets please.	**Vorrei dei biglietti di andata e ritorno.**	Vo-ray day beel-yet-tee dee andata e reetorno.
I want to come back today /tomorrow /in four days.	**Vorrei tornare oggi /domani. /tra quattro giorni.**	Vo-ray tornaray ojee /daw-mani /tra kwattro jornee
Do I have to change?	**Devo cambiare?**	Dayvo kambeearay?
Is there a fast train?	**C'è un rapido?**	Chay oon rapeedo?
What time does it arrive in…?	**A che ora arriva a…?**	A kay ora arreeva ah…?
Which platform does the train for… leave from?	**Da quale binario parte il treno per…?**	Da kwalay beenareeo partay eel trayno pair…?
Is there a connection to…?	**C'è una coincidenza per…?**	Chay oona coeencheedayntsa pair…?

... AT THE AIRPORT

English	Italian	Pronunciation
Can I buy a ticket to...?	Vorrei un biglietto per...	Vo-ray oon beel-yet-to pair...
Are there any supplements or taxes?	Ci sono supplementi o tasse aeroportuali da pagare?	Chee sono soopplaymayntee o tassay a-airoportwalee da pagaray?
I want an economy ticket.	Vorrei un biglietto in classe economica.	Vo-ray oon beel-yet-to een klassay ekonomika.
I want to fly business class.	Vorrei volare in business class.	Vo-ray volaray een business class.
Can I buy a ticket at the airport?	Posso comprare il biglietto all'aeroporto?	Posso kom-praray eel beel-yet-to ala-airoporto?
How can I get to the airport?	Come arrivo all'aeroporto?	Komay arreevo ala-airoporto?
What time must I check in?	A che ora devo fare il check-in?	A kay ora dayvo faray eel check-in?
Where is the check-in desk for flights to...?	Dove si fa il check-in dei voli per...?	Dovay see fa eel check-in day volee pair...?
Can I check in, please?	Vorrei fare il check-in, per favore.	Vo-ray faray eel check-in, pair fa-voray.
Could I have... /an aisle seat?	Vorrei... /un posto vicino al corridoio.	Vo-ray /oon posto veecheeno al korreedoeeo.
/a window seat?	/un posto vicino al finestrino.	/oon posto veecheeno al feenaystreeno.
Could I sit by the emergency exit?	Vorrei sedere vicino all'uscita di emergenza	Vo-ray saydairay veecheeno alloosheeta dee aymairjayntsa
Can I take this as hand luggage?	Posso portare questo come bagaglio a mano?	Posso portaray kwaysto komay baga-lyo ah mano?

USEFUL WORDS

airport	aeroporto	a-airoporto
arrivals	arrivi	arreevee
bag	borsa	borsa
book	libro	leebro
bus station	stazione degli autobus	statseeonay day-lyee owtoboos
bus stop	fermata d'autobus	fairmata dowtoboos
cancel	annullare	annullaray
change	cambiare	kambeea-ray
delay	ritardo	reetardo
departures	partenze	partaynzay
early	in anticipo	een anteecheepo
exit	uscita	oosheeta
hand luggage	bagaglio a mano	baga-lyo ah mano
late	in ritardo	een reetardo
luggage	bagagli	baga-lyee
map	pianta	peeanta
passport	passaporto	passaporto
place	posto	posto
reserve	riservare	risairvaray
road	strada	straada
rucksack	zaino	tsa-eeno
security check	ispezione di sicurezza	eespaytseeonay dee seekooraytsa
street name	nome della strada	nomay daylla straada

suitcase	valigia	valeeja
tax	tassa	tassa
taxi	taxi	taxi
ticket	biglietto	beel-yet-to
train station	stazione dei treni	statseeonay day traynee
underground/ subway	metropolitana	maytropoleetana
visa	visto	veesto
walk	camminare	kamminaray

RENTING A CAR

We have booked a rental car.	Abbiamo prenotato un'auto a noleggio.	Abbeeamo praynotato oon owto ah nolayjo.
🗣 Could we rent a car, please?	Vorremmo noleggiare un'auto, per favore	Vorraymmo nolayjaray oon owto, pair fa-voray
🗣 How much is it for... /a week? /a day?	Quanto costa per... /una settimana? /un giorno?	Kwanto kosta pair... /oona saytteemana? /oon jorno?
Does the price include insurance?	Il prezzo include l'assicurazione?	Eel praytso eenklooday lasseekoorat-seeonay?

English	Italian	Pronunciation
Is there anything else to pay?	Ci sono altre spese?	Chee sono aaltray spayzay?
Do I have to leave a deposit?	Devo versare una cauzione?	Dayvo versaray oona kowtseeonay?
Can I have a cheaper car?	Posso avere un'auto più economica?	Posso avairay oon owto peew ekonomika?
Can I have a bigger car?	Posso avere un'auto più grande?	Posso avairay oon owto peew graanday?
Can we have a car with a radio?	Possiamo avere un'auto con la radio?	Posseeamo avairay oon owto kon la radeeo?
Which number do we call if we break down?	Quale numero dobbiamo chiamare in caso di guasto?	Kwalay noo-may-ro dobbeeamo kea-maray een kazo dee gwasto?
What sort of petrol does it take?	Che tipo di benzina ci vuole?	Kay teepo dee baynteseena chee vwolay?
Where do we return the car?	Dove dobbiamo riportare l'auto?	Dovay dobbeeamo riportaray lowto?
Can we leave the car at the airport?	Possiamo lasciare l'auto in aeroporto?	Posseeamo lashiaaray lowto een a-airoporto?
Where is the car?	Dov'è l'auto?	Doveh lowto?

HEARING

English	Italian	Pronunciation
Can I see your licence?	Mi fa vedere la sua patente?	Mee fa vedairay la swa patayntay?
You must leave a deposit.	Deve lasciare una cauzione.	Dayvay lashiaaray oona kowtseeonay.
How long do you want the car?	Per quanto tempo vuole l'auto?	Pair kwanto taympo vwolay lowto?
This is the number to call if you have a problem.	Questo è il numero da chiamare se ci sono problemi.	Kwaysto eh eel noo-may-ro da keea-maray say chee sono problaymee.

DRIVING

Is this the right road for...?	È la strada giusta per...?	Eh la straada joosta pair...?
How do I get to the motorway?	Come arrivo all'autostrada?	Komay arreevo allowto-straada?
How far is it?	Quanto dista?	Kwanto deesta?

Where is the nearest petrol station?	Dov'è il distributore di benzina più vicino?	Doveh eel deestreebootoray dee bayntseena pew veecheeno?
Full tank, please.	Il pieno, per favore.	Eel peeayno pair fa-voray.
I want to pay for the petrol on pump number...	Vorrei pagare la benzina della pompa numero...	Vo-ray pagaray la bayntseena daylla pompa noo-may-ro...
Where are the air and water?	Dove sono la pompa dell'aria e dell'acqua?	Dovay sono la pompa dell areea ay dayll akwa?
Where can I park?	Dove posso parcheggiare?	Dovay posso parkayjaray
How much is it to park here?	Quanto costa parcheggiare qui?	Kwanto kosta parkayjaray kwee?

PROBLEMS

Can you help me? I've broken down.	Mi può aiutare? Ho un guasto alla machina.	Mee pwo ah-u-taray? O oon gwasto al-la makkina.
Can you help me? I've run out of petrol.	Mi può aiutare? Ho finito la benzina.	Mee pwo ah-u-taray? Oh fee-neeto la bayntseena.
I've had an accident.	Ho avuto un incidente.	Oavo oto oon eencheedayntay.

My car has been stolen.	Mi hanno rubato la macchina.	Mee anno roobato la makkina.
The windscreen is broken.	Il parabrezza è rotto.	Eel parabraytsa eh rotto.
Thanks for your help.	Grazie per l'aiuto.	Gratseeay pair lah-u-toh.

USEFUL WORDS

accident	incidente	eencheedayntay
air conditioning	aria condizionata	areea kondeetseeonata
breakdown	guasto	gwasto
brakes	freni	fraynee
car park	parcheggio	parkayjo
clutch	frizione	freetseeonay
diesel	diesel	diesel
exhaust	scappamento	skappamaynto
keys	chiavi	keeavee
licence	patente	patayntay
lock	serratura	serratoora
oil	olio	oleo
overheating	surriscaldamento	soor-reeskaldamaynto
petrol	benzina	bayntseena
puncture	foratura	foratoora
radiator	radiatore	radeeatoray
tyre	pneumatico	pnay-oomateeko
water	acqua	akwa

STAYING THE NIGHT

HOTELS AND GUESTHOUSES
CHECKING IN

I have a reservation.	Ho una prenotazione.	Oh oona praynotatseonay.
Do you have a room for tonight?	Avete una camera per stanotte?	Avaytay oona camera pair stanottay?
I want a room for...	Vorrei una camera per...	Vo-ray oona camera pair...
/one night.	/una notte.	/oona nottay.
/three nights.	/tre notti.	/tray notti.
/one week.	/una settimana.	/oona sayttemana.
How much is the room?	Quanto costa la camera?	Kwanto kosta la camera?
Do you have a cheaper room?	Avete una stanza meno costosa?	Avaytay oona stantsa mayno kostoza?
Does the price include breakfast?	La colazione è inclusa?	La colatseeonay eh eenklooza?
Can I pay with a credit card?	Posso pagare con carta di credito?	Posso pagaray kon karta dee kraydito?
Can I have my key, please? I'm in room...	Vorrei la mia chiave, per favore. Sono nella stanza...	Vo-ray la meea keeavay pair fa-voray. Sono naylla stantsa...

CHECKING OUT

What time must I check out?	A che ora devo lasciare la camera?	A kay ora dayvo lashiaaray la kaamaira?
Can I have a taxi for... o'clock?	Vorrei un taxi per le...	Vo-ray oon taxi pair lay...
Can I pay the bill please?	Vorrei pagare il conto.	Vo-ray pagaray eel konto.

HEARING

How many people?	Quante persone siete?	Kwantay pair-sonay seeaytay?
How long do you want to stay?	Quanto vi volete fermare?	Kwanto vee volaytay fermaaray?
Do you have luggage?	Avete bagagli?	Avaytay baga-lyee?
Can I see your passport, please?	I vostri passaporti, per favore.	Ee vostri passaporti, pair fa-voray.
Do you have a reservation?	Avete una prenotazione?	Avaytay oona praynotatseonay?
Sorry, we're full.	Mi dispiace, siamo al completo.	Mee dispeea-chay seeamo al complayto.
No vacancies.	Completo.	Complayto.

ASKING FOR WHAT YOU WANT

I'd like...	Vorrei...	Vo-ray...
/a single room.	/una camera singola.	/oona camera seengola
/a double room.	/una camera doppia.	/oona camera doppeea
I'd like a room with a bathroom.	Vorrei una camera con bagno.	Vo-ray oona camera kon banyo.
I'd like a family room for two adults and one child/two children.	Vorrei una camera familiare, per due adulti e un bambino/ due bambini.	Vo-ray oona camera familiaray, pair dooay adoolti e oon bambeeno/ dooay bambeeni
I'd like twin beds.	Vorrei due letti singoli.	Vo-ray dooay laytti seengoli.
Can I have a room away from the street?	Vorrei una stanza che non si affaccia sulla strada.	Vo-ray oona stantsa kay non see affacha soolla straada.
Can I have a room with a view?	Vorrei una camera con vista panoramica.	Vo-ray oona camera kon veesta panoramika.
What time is breakfast?	A che ora servite la colazione?	A kay ora sairveetay la colatseeonay?
What time is the front door locked?	A che ora chiudete il portone?	A kay ora keeoodaytay eel portonay?
Will there be someone to let us in at... o'clock?	C'è qualcuno per poter rientrare alle...?	Chay kwalkoono pair potair re-entraray allay...?
Is there a swimming pool here?	C'è una piscina?	Chay oona peesheena?
Is there a restaurant in the hotel?	C'è un ristorante nell'albergo?	Chay oon reestorantay nayllalbairgo?
Can I have a cot for our baby?	Potrei avere una culla o un lettino per il bambino?	Potray avairay oona kool-la o oon laytteeno pair eel bambeeno?
Can I leave this in the hotel safe?	Posso lasciare questo nella cassaforte dell'albergo?	Posso lashiaaray kwaysto naylla cassa-fortay dayll albairgo?

English	Italian	Pronunciation
Where can I make a phone call?	Dove posso fare una telefonata?	Dovay posso faray oona taylayfonata?
Can I have breakfast in my room?	Si può avere la colazione in camera?	See pwo avairay la colatseeonay een camera?
Can we leave our luggage?	Possiamo lasciare i bagagli?	Posseeamo lashiaaray ee baga-lyee?
Are there any messages for me?	Ci sono messaggi per me?	Chee sono mayssajee pair may?
Can I leave a message for…	Vorrei lasciare un messaggio per…	Vo-ray lashiaaray oon messajo pair…

PROBLEMS

English	Italian	Pronunciation
There is no hot water.	Non c'è acqua calda.	Non chay akwa kaalda
The light/the tv doesn't work.	La luce/ la televisione non funziona.	La loochay/la taylayveezeeonay non foontseeona.
I can't open the window.	La finestra non si apre.	La feenaystra non see apray.
I've lost my key.	Ho perso la chiave.	Oh pairso la keeavay.
I'm locked out of my room.	Sono rimasto chiuso fuori dalla stanza.	Sono reemasto keeoozo fwori dalla stantsa.

English	Italian	Pronunciation
The door won't lock.	La porta non si chiude a chiave.	La porta non see keeooday ah keeavay.
My room needs cleaning.	La mia stanza deve essere pulita.	La meea stantsa dayvay ayssairay pooleeta.
Could we have…	Vorremmo…	Vorraymmo…
/clean towels?	/degli asciugamani puliti.	/day-lyee asheeoogamanee pooleetee.
/clean bedding?	/delle lenzuola pulite.	/dayllay laynytswola pooleetay.
/another pillow?	/un altro cuscino.	/oonaaltro koosheeno.
My room is too noisy.	La mia stanza è troppo rumorosa.	La meea stantsa eh trop-po roomoroza.
Can we have a different room?	Possiamo avere un'altra camera?	Posseeamo avairay oonaaltra kaamaira?
My room is too cold/hot.	La mia stanza è troppo fredda/calda.	La meea stantsa eh troppofrayd-da/kaalda.
I think this bill is wrong – could you check it, please?	Credo che questo conto sia sbagliato – può controllarlo, per favore?	Kraydo kay kwaysto konto seea sba-lyato – pwo kontro-laarlo pair fa-voray?

RENTING AND APARTMENTS

Where is the reception?	Dov'è la reception?	Doveh la reception?
Where can I collect the key?	Dove posso prendere la chiave?	Dovay posso prayndairay la keeaway?
Can I see the apartment?	Posso vedere l'appartamento?	Posso vedairay lappartamaynto?
How much is the rent for... days?	Quanto costa l'appartamento per... giorni?	Kwanto kosta l'appartamaynto pair... jornee?
Where can I buy...	Dove posso comprare del...	Dovay posso kom-praray dayl...
/milk?	/latte?	/lattay?
/gas?	/gas?	/gaz?
/bread?	/pane?	/panay?
Where does the rubbish go?	Dove si butta la spazzatura?	Dovay see boot-ta la spatsatoora?
Can you show me how to work...	Vorrei vedere come funziona...	Vo-ray vedairay komay funtseeona...
/the cooker?	/il fornello.	/eel fornayllo.
/the heating?	/il riscaldamento.	/eel reeskald-amaynto.
/the hot water?	/l'acqua calda.	/lakwa kaalda.
/the washing machine?	/la lavatrice.	/la lava-treechay.
Can we have more bedding?	Possiamo avere delle altre coperte?	Possee-amo aavairay del-lay aaltray kopayrtay?

USEFUL WORDS

apartment	appartamento	appartamaynto
balcony	balcone	baalkonay
bathroom	bagno	banyo
bed and breakfast	bed and breakfast	bed and breakfast
blanket	coperta	kopairta
cooker	fornello	fornayllo
cork screw	cavatappi	kavatappi
cutlery	posate	pozaatay
day	giorno	jorno
dinner	cena	chayna
fridge	frigo	freego
full board	pensione completa	payntseeonay komplayta
guest house	foresteria	foraystaireea
gym	palestra	palaystra
half board	mezza pensione	maytsa payntseeonay

hangers	**attaccapanni**	attakkapanni
hotel	**hotel**	ohtel
key	**chiave**	keeaavy
lift	**ascensore**	ashaynsoray
light	**luce**	loochay
lunch	**pranzo**	prantso
playground	**parco giochi**	paarko jo-kee
plug	**spina elettrica**	speena aylayttreeka
reception	**reception**	reception
room	**stanza**	stantsa
sauna	**sauna**	sowna
shower	**doccia**	dotcha
soap	**sapone**	saponay
swimming pool	**piscina**	peesheena
television	**televisione**	taylayveezeeonay
tin opener	**apriscatole**	apreeskatolay
towel	**asciugamano**	asheeoogamano
week	**settimana**	saytteemana

CAMPING AND CARAVANNING

Where is the nearest campsite?	**Dov'è il campeggio più vicino?**	Doveh eel kampayjo peew veecheeno?
I have booked a pitch.	**Ho prenotato una piazzola.**	Oh praynotato oona peeatsola.
Where do we go?	**Dove andiamo?**	Dovay andeeamo?
Can we put our caravan/tent here?	**Possiamo mettere la nostra roulotte/ tenda qui?**	Posseeamo mayttairay la nostra roulotte/ tenda kwee?

ASKING FOR WHAT YOU WANT

Could we have a different pitch?	**Possiamo avere un'altra piazzola?**	Posseeamo avairay oonaaltra peeatsola?
We'd like some shade.	**Vorremmo un po' d'ombra.**	Vorraymmo oon po dombra.
Are there any power points?	**Ci sono delle prese elettriche?**	Chee sono dayllay prayzay aylayttreekay?
When does the shop open?	**Quando apre il negozio?**	Kwando apray eel naygotseeo?
/close?	**/chiude il negozio?**	/keeooday eel naygotseeo?

Where is the drinking water?	**Dov'è l'acqua potabile?**	Doveh lakwa potabeelay?
Is there a swimming pool on site?	**Avete una piscina?**	Avaytay oona peesheena?
Where are...	**Dove sono...**	Dovay sono...
/the showers?	**/le docce?**	/lay dotchay?
/the toilets?	**/i bagni?**	/ee banyee?
Is there somewhere I can dry clothes /wash clothes?	**Dove posso asciugare la biancheria /lavare la biancheria?**	Dovay posso asheeoogaray la beeankereea lavaray la beeankereea?
Where can I get gas?	**Dove posso trovare il gas?**	Dovay posso tro-varay eel gaz?

USEFUL WORDS

barbecue	**barbecue**	barbecue
camp fire	**fornello da campo**	fornayllo da kampo
caravan	**roulotte**	roulotte
cooker	**fornello**	fornayllo
drinking water	**acqua potabile**	akwa potabeelay
fire	**fuoco**	fwoko
gas	**gas**	gaz
kitchen	**cucina**	koocheena
matches	**fiammiferi**	feeammeeferi
pegs	**picchetti**	peekkaytti
rubbish	**spazzatura**	spatsatoora
showers	**docce**	dotchay
sleeping bag	**sacco a pelo**	sakko ah paylo
tent	**tenda**	tenda
washing line	**filo per stendere il bucato**	feelo pair stayndairay eel bookato

LEISURE AND SPORT

LEISURE
ASKING FOR WHAT YOU WANT

How much does it cost to get in?	Quanto costa il biglietto d'ingresso?	Kwanto kosta eel beel-yet-to dingresso?
Is there a discount for...	Ci sono sconti per...	Chee sono skonti pair...
/students?	/studenti?	/stoodaynti?
/children?	/bambini?	/bambeeni?
Is there anything for children to do?	Ci sono attività o giochi per i bambini?	Chee sono atteeveeta o jo-kee pair ee bambeeni?
Is there a guided tour?	Si può fare una visita guidata?	See pwo faray oona visita gwee-daata?
Can we go inside?	Possiamo entrare?	Posseeamo en-traray?
Is it open all week?	È aperto tutta la settimana?	Eh apairto tootta la saytteemana?
Where is the tourist information?	Dov'è l'ufficio del turismo?	Doveh loof-feecheeo dayl tooreezmo?
Can I have a map of the city?	Posso avere una pianta della città?	Posso avairay oona peeanta daylla chee-ta?
Can you show me where I am?	Può mostrarmi dove sono?	Pwo mostrarmee dovay sono?

How can I get there?	Come posso arrivarci?	Komay posso arree-varchee?
What are the best things to see?	Quali sono le cose più interessanti da vedere?	Qwalee sono le kozay peew eenteray-santee da vedairay?
I like...	Mi piace...	Mee peea-chay
/art.	/l'arte.	/lartay.
/architecture.	/l'architettura.	/larkeetayttoora
/shopping.	/fare shopping.	/faray shopping
/boat trips.	/fare gite in battello.	/faray geeteh een battayllo.
/history.	/la storia.	la storia.
Can you suggest a good day trip?	Mi può suggerire una bella gita di un giorno?	Mee pwo soojaireeray oona bella jeeta dee oon jorno?
Do you have a calendar of events?	Avete un calendario delle manifestazioni in programma?	Avaytay oon kalayndareeo dayl-lay maneefaystat-seeonee een programma?
Is there anything for children?	C'è qualcosa per i bambini?	Chay kwalkoza pair ee bambeeni?
When are the markets?	Quando ci sono i mercati?	Kwando chee sono ee mair-katee?

HEARING

How many tickets do you want?	**Quanti biglietti desidera?**	Kwantee beel-yet-tee dezeedaira?
The boat/bus leaves in five minutes/at 3 o'clock.	**Il battello/ autobus parte tra cinque minuti/ alle quindici.**	Eel battayllo/ owtoboos partay tra cheenkway meenootee/allay kweendeechee.
We close at 6pm.	**Chiudiamo alle diciotto.**	Keeoodeeamo allay deechotto.
We open at 10am.	**Apriamo alle dieci.**	Apreeamo allay deeaychee.

USEFUL WORDS

admission	**entrata**	entraata
bridge	**ponte**	pontay
castle	**castello**	kastayllo
cathedral	**cattedrale**	kattay-dralay
cemetery	**cimitero**	cheemeetairo
church	**chiesa**	keeayza
closed	**chiuso**	keeoozo
ferry	**traghetto**	tragaytto
gallery	**galleria**	gallaireeya
guide	**guida**	gweeda
hotel	**hotel**	ohtel
museum	**museo**	moozayo
old town	**centro storico**	chayntro sto-riko

opening hours	**orario d'apertura**	orareeo dapairtoora
palace	**palazzo**	palatso
park	**parco**	parko
river	**fiume**	feeoomay
river trip	**gita sul fiume**	jeeta sool feeoomay
shopping mall	**centro commerciale**	chayntro kommer-chialay
statue	**statua**	statwa
tower	**torre**	torray
tour	**visita**	visita
zoo	**zoo**	tso

SPORT
ASKING FOR WHAT YOU WANT

Where can we hire bicycles?	**Dove possiamo noleggiare delle biciclette?**	Dovay pos-seeamo nolejaray dayllay beecheeclayttay?
Where can we go walking?	**Dove possiamo andare a fare una passeggiata?**	Dovay pos-seeamo andaray ah faray oona passejaataa?
Is there a path/ a cycle path?	**C'è un percorso/ una pista ciclabile?**	Chay oon pairko-rso/oona peesta cheeclabeelay?

Where can we...	Dove possiamo...	Dovay posseeamo...
/play tennis?	/giocare a tennis?	/jokaray ah tennis?
/play golf?	/giocare a golf?	/jokaray ah golf?
/play pool?	/giocare a biliardo?	/jokaray ah beeleeardo?
/go ice skating?	/andare a pattinare sul ghiaccio?	/an-daray ah pattee-naray sool gheeacho?
/go swimming?	/andare a nuotare?	/an-daray ah nwo-taray?
Can I hire /equipment?	Vorrei noleggiare /l'attrezzatura.	Vo-ray nolay-jaray /lattraytsatoora.
/a racket?	/una racchetta.	/oona rakkaytta.
/clubs?	/le mazze da golf.	/lay matsay da golf.
Where can we see /football?	Dove possiamo vedere /una partita di calcio?	Dovay posseeamo vedairay /oona parteeta dee kaalchio?
/horse racing?	/le corse di cavalli?	/lay korsay dee kavalli?
Who's playing?	Chi sta giocando?	Kee sta jokando?
Where can we get tickets?	Dove possiamo acquistare i biglietti?	Dovay posseeamo aakweestaaray ee beel-yet-tee?

USEFUL WORDS

bait	esca	ayska
club	club (social)/ mazza da golf (sport)	club/matsa da golf
fishing rod	canna da pesca	kanna da payska
fly fishing	pesca	payska
football	calcio	kaalchio
golf	golf	golf
gym	palestra	palaystra
join	diventare membro di	deevayntaray maymbro dee
point	punto	poonto
racket	racchetta	rakkaytta
score	segnare un punto	senyaray oon poonto
sauna	sauna	sowna
swimming pool	piscina	peesheena
tennis	tennis	tennis

EATING OUT

SNACKS CAFÉS AND BARS

Excuse me, waiter!	Scusi, cameriere!	Skoozee, kamaireeairay!
I'd like...	Vorrei...	Vo-ray...
/a beer.	/una birra.	/oona beerra.
/coffee.	/un caffè.	/oon ka-fay.
/coffee with milk.	/un caffè con latte.	/oon ka-fay kon lattay.
/tea with milk.	/un tè con latte.	/oon te kon lattay.
/orange juice.	/un succo d'arancia.	/oon sookko d'arantcha.
/mineral water.	/dell'acqua minerale.	/dell akwa mineraaly.
Can we sit here?	Possiamo sederci qui?	Possee-amo saydairchee kwee?
What soft drinks do you have?	Che bibite analcoliche avete?	Kay beebeetay analkoleekay avaytay?
Another drink, please.	Ci porta ancora qualcosa da bere, per favore?	Chee portaa aankora kwalkoza da bairay pair fa-voray?
The same again, please.	Un'altra, per favore.	Oonaaltra pair fa-voray.
What snacks do you have?	Che cosa avete per fare uno spuntino?	Kay koza avaytay pair faray oono spoonteeno?
Do you sell cigarettes?	Vendete sigarette?	Vendaytay seegarayttay?
Where are the toilets?	Dove sono i bagni?	Dovay sono ee banyee?
Can I have the bill, please?	Ma fa il conto, per favore?	Mee fa eel konto pair favoray?

HEARING AND READING

What can I get you?	Cosa posso portarle?	Koza posso por-tarlay?
What would you like?	Cosa prende?	Koza praynday?
Would you like anything else?	Desidera altro?	Dezeedaira aaltro?
What would you like...	Cosa vuole...	Koza vwolay...
/to drink?	/da bere?	/da bairay?
/to eat?	/da mangiare?	/da man-jaray?
The specials are on the board.	I piatti del giorno sono sulla lavagna.	Ee peeattee dayl jorno sono soolla lavanya.
Service included.	Servizio incluso.	Sairveetseeo eenkloozo.
Service not included.	Servizio non incluso.	Sairveetseeo non eenkloozo.
Smoking/ non-smoking.	Fumatori/ non fumatori.	Foomatori/ non foomatori.

USEFUL WORDS

a lot	**molto**	molto
a little	**poco**	poko
beer	**birra**	beerra
– white	**– chiara**	keeara
– red	**– rossa**	rossa
– dark	**– scura**	skoora
bill	**conto**	konto
bottle of/	**una bottiglia**	oona bottee-lya
half bottle of	**di/mezza**	dee/maytsa
	bottiglia di	bottee-lya dee
brandy	**brandy**	brandy
breakfast	**colazione**	colatseeonay
cider	**sidro**	seedro
cocktail	**cocktail**	cocktail
gin	**gin**	gin
inside	**dentro**	dayntro
lager	**lager**	lager
lunch	**pranzo**	prantso
one litre/	**un litro/**	oon leetro/
half litre	**mezzo litro**	maytso leetro
menu	**menu**	menoo
outside	**fuori**	fwori
peanuts	**noccioline**	notcho-leenay
port	**porto**	porto
rum	**rum**	room
snack	**snack/spuntino**	snack/ spoonteeno
sparkling	**frizzante**	freetsantay

table	**tavolo**	tavolo
tap water	**acqua del**	akwa dayl
	rubinetto	roobeenaytto
whisky	**whisky**	whisky
wine	**vino**	veeno

RESTAURANTS

⏺ Do you have a table?	**Avete un tavolo libero?**	Avaytay oon tavolo leebairo?
Can we sit here?	**Possiamo sederci qui?**	Posseeamo saydairchee kwee?
⏺ A table for two/four, please.	**Un tavolo per due/quattro, per favore.**	Oon tavolo pair dooay/kwattro pair fa-voray.
⏺ Do you take credit cards?	**Accettate carte di credito?**	Achettaa-tay kartay dee kraydito?
Can we reserve a table for...	**Possiamo prenotare un tavolo per...**	Posseeamo prayno-taray oon tavolo pair
/later?	**/dopo?**	/dopo?
/this evening?	**/questa sera?**	/kwaysta saira?
/tomorrow?	**/domani?**	/daw-mani?

Can we see the menu?	Possiamo vedere il menu?	Posseeamo vedairay eel menoo?
What are the specials?	Quali sono i piatti del giorno?	Kwalee sono ee peeattee dayl jorno?
I'd like... /the special.	Vorrei... /il piatto del giorno.	Vo-ray... /eel peeatto dayl jorno?
What's in this?	Cosa c'è in questo piatto?	Koza chay een kwaysto peatto?
How is this cooked?	Come viene preparato?	Komay veeay-nay prayparato?
Is this spicy?	È speziato?	Eh spetseeato?
Is this hot?	È piccante?	Eh pee-kantay?
Does this come with...	Questo piatto viene servito con...	Kwaysto peeatto veeaynay sairveeto kon...
/salad?	/insalata?	/insa-lata?
/chips?	/patatine fritte?	/patateenay freettay?
/vegetables?	/verdure?	/verdoo-ray?
/sauce?	/una salsa?	/oona saalsa?
Can I have a high chair, please?	Vorrei una seggiolone, per favore.	Vo-ray oon sayjo-lonay, pair fa-voray.
Can I have a child's portion, please?	Vorrei una porzione per bambini, per favore.	Vo-ray oona portseeonay pair bambeeni, pair fa-voray.

Is service included?	Il servizio è incluso?	Eel serveetseeo eh eenkloozo?
That was very good.	Era buonissimo.	Era bwonissimo.

HEARING

Can I take your coat?	Vuole darmi il suo cappotto?	Vwolay darmee el swo kappotto?
A table for two?	Un tavolo per due?	Oon tavolo pair dooay?
What would you like to drink?	Cosa prendete da bere?	Koza prayndaytay da bairay?
What can I get you?	Cosa vi porto?	Koza vee porto?

PROBLEMS

How much longer will the food be?	Quanto c'è da aspettare?	Kwanto chay da aspayttaray?
Could you get us a drink while we're waiting?	Potrebbe portarci da bere mentre aspettiamo?	Potraybbay portarchee da bairay mayntray aspaytteeamo?
Could we have some bread while we're waiting?	Potremmo avere del pane mentre aspettiamo?	Potraymmo avairay dayl panay mayntray aspaytteeamo?
This isn't what I ordered.	Non è quello che ho ordinato.	Non eh kwayllo kay oh ordeenato.

This tastes odd.	**Ha un sapore strano.**	Ah oon saporay strano.
My food is cold.	**Questo è freddo.**	Kwaysto eh frayddo.
I don't have my wallet.	**Non ho il portafoglio.**	Non oh eel portafo-lyo.
I don't have enough money with me.	**Non ho abbastanza denaro con me.**	Non oh abbastantsa daynaro kon may.

READING THE MENU

anchovies	**acciughe**	achoo-ghay
artichoke	**carciofo**	kartchofo
bacon	**pancetta**	panchaytta
baked	**al forno**	al forno
beef	**manzo**	mandzo
beans	**fagioli**	faj-olee
boiled	**bollito**	bolleeto
bread	**pane**	panay
braised	**stufato/brasato**	stoofato/brasato
butter	**burro**	boorro
cabbage	**cavolo**	kavolo
carrots	**carote**	karotay
cheese	**formaggio**	formajo
– goats cheese	**– caprino**	kapreeno
– blue cheese	**– erborinato**	airboreenato
chicken	**pollo**	pollo
chips	**patatine fritte**	patateenay freetay
chops	**costolette**	kostolayttay
coffee	**caffè**	ka-fay

cold	**freddo**	frayddo
course	**portata**	por-tata
crab	**granchio**	grankeeo
cream	**panna**	panna
duck	**anatra**	anatra
dumplings	**gnocchi**	nyokee
eggs	**uova**	wova
fish	**pesce**	payshay
flan	**timballo/ sformato**	teemballo/ sformato
fried	**fritto**	freetto
garlic	**aglio**	a-lyo
goose	**oca**	oka
gravy	**sugo**	soogo
green beans	**fagiolini**	fajoleeni
ham	**prosciutto**	proshootto
heart	**cuore**	kworay
honey	**miele**	meeaylay
horse	**cavallo**	kavallo
hot	**caldo (temperature)/ piccante (spicy)**	kaaldo/ pee-kantay
jam	**marmellata**	marmay-lata
jelly	**gelatina**	jaylateena
kidney	**rognone**	ronyonay
lamb	**vitello**	veetayllo
leek	**porro**	porro

lentils	lenticchie	laynteekkeeay
liver	fegato	fay-gato
lobster	aragosta	aragosta
loin	lombo	lombo
main course	piatto	peeatto
	principale	preenchee-palay
marinated	marinato	mareenato
mussels	cozze	cotse
mutton	montone	montonay
olive oil	olio d'oliva	oleo doleeva
oysters	ostriche	ostreekay
pancakes	pancakes	pancakes
pâté	patè	pa-tay
pasta	pasta	pasta
pastry	pasticcino	pastcheeno
peas	piselli	peesaylli
pie	torta	torta
poached	in camicia	een kameecha
pork	maiale	ma-yalay
potatoes/	patate/	pa-tatay/
– mashed	purè di	pooray dee
	patate	pa-tatay
– fried	patate fritte	pa-tatay freettay
– chipped	patatine	patateenay
– boiled	patate lesse	pa-tatay lessay
– roast	patate arrosto	pa-tatay arrosto
pudding	budino	boodeeno
rabbit	coniglio	konee-lyo
red beans	fagioli rossi	faj-olee rossee
rice	riso	reeso

roast	arrosto	arrosto
rolls	panini	paneeni
salad	insalata	insa-lata
sauce	salsa	saalsa
sausage	salsiccia	salseecha
seafood	frutti di	frootti dee
	mare	maray
snails	lumache	loo-makay
soup	zuppa	tsooppa
spicy	speziato	spetseeato
starter	antipasto	anteepasto
steak	bistecca	beestaykka
stewed	stufato	stoofato
tea	tè	tay
toast	toast	toast
tomatoes	pomodori	pomodori
tripe	trippa	treeppa
trout	trota	trota
tuna	tonno	tonno
veal	vitello	veetayllo
vegetables	verdure	verdoo-ray
water (still)	acqua	akwa
	(naturale)	(natu-ra-lay)
water (fizzy)	acqua	akwa
	(frizzante)	(free-tsantay)
wine (white)	vino (bianco)	veeno
		(beeanko)
wine (red)	vino (rosso)	veeno (rosso)
wine (table)	vino	veeno
	(da tavola)	(da tavola)

BUSINESS

INTRODUCTIONS & GREETINGS

How are you?	**Come sta?**	Komay sta?
Delighted to meet you.	**Lieto (M)/ Lieta (F) di conoscerla.**	Leeayto/ leeayta dee konoshairla.
Nice to see you again.	**Lieto (M)/Lieta (F) di rivederla.**	Leeayto/leeayta dee reevaydairla.
Let me introduce my colleague.	**Le presento il mio (M)/la mia (F) collega.**	Lay prayzaynto eel meeo/la meea kollayga.
This is...	**Si chiama...**	See keeaama...

ASKING FOR WHAT YOU WANT

Can you show me...	**Vorrei vedere...**	Vo-ray vedairay...
/designs.	**/i disegni.**	/ee deesaynyee.
/pictures.	**/le foto.**	/lay foto.
/figures.	**/i dati.**	/ee dati.
/projections.	**/le proiezioni.**	/lay proeeayt-seeonee.
/the new line.	**/la nuova linea.**	/la nwova leenaya
When will these be ready?	**Quando saranno pronti?**	Kwando saran-no prontee?
Could you repeat that?	**Può ripetere, per favore?**	Pwo reepaytairay, pair fa-voray?

I'd like to check...	**Vorrei controllare...**	Vo-ray kontro-laray...
/the sizes.	**/le misure.**	/lay mizooray.
/the colours.	**/i colori.**	/ee kolori.
I'd like to make an order for...	**Vorrei ordinare...**	Vo-ray ordi-naray...
Would you send me...?	**Può spedirmi...?**	Pwo spaydeermi...?
We need...	**Abbiamo bisogno di...**	Abbeeamo beezonyo dee...
/more time.	**/più tempo.**	/peew taympo.
/more information.	**/più informazioni.**	/peew eenformat-seeoni.
/a better idea of what you need.	**/un'idea più precisa su quello che le serve.**	/ooneedaya peew pray-cheeza soo kwayllo kay le servay.

INFORMATION AND DISCUSSING BUSINESS

We have different sizes /colours. | Abbiamo diverse misure /diversi colori. | Abbeeamo divairsay mizooray deevairsee kolori
Would you like to see some samples? | Vuole vedere qualche campione? | Vwolay vedairay kwalkay kampeeonay?
I can leave these with you. I will check the delivery dates for you. | Posso lasciarle questi. Controllerò la data di consegna per lei. | Posso lasheearlay kwaystee. Kontrollairo la daata dee konsaynya pair lay.
Thank you for your order. I can come back to you with a price later. | Grazie per il Suo ordine. Posso comunicarle il prezzo più tardi. | Gratseeay pair eel swo ordeenay. Posso komooni-karlay eel praytso peew tardee.
This is our best price. | Questo è il nostro miglior prezzo. | Kwaysto eh eel nostro mee-lyor praytso
This price is in Euros. We can offer you credit terms. | Questo è il prezzo in Euro. Possiamo offrirle un pagamento dilazionato. | Kwaysto eh eel praytso een ayooro Posseeamo offreerlay oon pagamaynto deelatseonato.
This price includes delivery. | Questo prezzo include la consegna. | Kwaysto prayt-so eenklooday la konsaynya.

We need payment before sending the goods. | Abbiamo bisogno di ricevere il pagamento prima di inviare la merce. | Abbeeamo beezonyo dee reechayvairay eel pagamaynto preema dee invee-aray la mair-chay.
We accept credit cards or bank transfers. | Accettiamo carte di credito e bonifici bancari. | Achaytteeyamo kartay dee kraydito ay boneefeechee bankari.
We can send these/it straight away. | Possiamo inviare questa merce immediatamente. | Posseeamo invee-aray kwaysta mair-chay eemmay-deeatamayntay.
/next week. | /la prossima settimana. | /la prossima saytteemana.
/next month. | /il mese prossimo. | /eel mayzay prossimo.
We have some point of sale material. | Abbiamo del materiale promozionale illustrativo. | Abbeeamo dayl matay-realay promotseeo-nalay eelloostrateevo.
I need to check that with my colleagues. | Devo controllare con i miei colleghi. | Dayvo kontro-laray kon ee meeay kollay-ghee

/with head office.	/con la sede centrale.	/kon la saiday chentraalay.
/the warehouse.	/con il magazzino.	/kon eel magatseeno.
Shall we talk about...	Possiamo parlare di...	Posseeamo parlaray dee...
/prices?	/prezzi?	/praytsee?
/terms?	/condizioni?	/kondeetseeoni?
/credit?	/credito?	/kraydito?
/delivery dates?	/date di consegna?	/datay dee konsaynya?
Can we talk about...	Possiamo parlare...	Posseeamo parlaray
/the brief?	/delle istruzioni?	/dayllay eestrootseeonee?
/your needs?	/delle sue necessità?	/dayllay sway naychayssee-ta?
/the audience?	/di utenti finali?	/dee ootenti fi-nali?
/the targets?	/di obiettivi?	/dee obeeaytteevi?
/alternatives?	/delle alternative?	/dayllay altairnateevay?
/the competition?	/della concorrenza?	/daylla konkorrayntsa?
I would like some information about...	Vorrei delle informazioni su...	Vo-ray dayllay eenformatseeonee soo...
I would like to know about...	Vorrei sapere...	Vo-ray sapairay...

AGREEING AND DISAGREEING

That's a good idea.	Questa è una buona idea.	Kwaysta eh oona bwona eedaya.
That's an excellent idea.	Questa è un'ottima idea.	Kwaysta eh oonotteema eedaya.
I like this/ it very much.	Mi piace molto.	Mee peea-chay molto
It's not bad.	Non è male.	Non eh maalay.
I don't like this /it at all.	Non mi piace per niente.	Non mee peea-chay pair neeayntay
It's nothing special.	Non è niente di speciale.	Non eh neeayntay dee spay-cha-lay.
It's not possible.	Non è possibile.	Non eh possee-beelay.
I agree entirely.	Sono pienamente d'accordo.	Sono peeayna-mayntay dakkordo.
I really don't agree.	Non sono assolutamente d'accordo.	Non sono assoloota-mayntay dakkordo.
No, not necessarily.	No, non necessariamente.	No non nay-chayssaree-mayntay.
I have another meeting in...	Ho un'altra riunione fra...	Oh oonaaltra reeooneeonay fra...
/half an hour.	/mezz'ora.	/maytsora.
/after this one.	/dopo questa.	/dopo kwaysta.

Shall we meet again later?	**Possiamo incontrarci di nuovo più tardi?**	Posseeamo eenkontrarchee dee nwovo peew tardee?
Can we put it off till tomorrow?	**Possiamo rimandare a domani?**	Posseeamo reemaandaaray ah daw-mani?
Ok, see you later.	**Bene, a più tardi allora.**	Baynay, ah peew tardee allora.
What about tomorrow?	**Le andrebbe bene domani?**	Lay andraybbay baynay daw-mani?

USEFUL WORDS

agreement	**accordo**	akkordo
brief	**istruzioni**	eestrootseeonee
busy	**occupato**	okkoopato
buying	**acquisto**	akweesto
colour	**colore**	koloray
competitor	**concorrente**	konkorrayntay

credit	**credito**	kraydito
customer	**cliente**	kleeayntay
customs	**dogana**	dogana
deadline	**scadenza**	scadentsa
delivery	**consegna**	konsaynya
design	**disegno/ progetto**	deesaynyo/ projaytto
idea	**idea**	eedaya
market	**mercato**	mairkato
material	**materiale**	mataireealay
meeting	**meeting/ riunione**	meeting /reeooneeonay
product	**prodotto**	prodotto
quality	**qualità**	kwali-ta
report	**rapporto**	rapporto
sale	**vendita**	vayndita
samples	**campioni**	kampeeoni
size	**misura**	meezoora
terms	**termini/ condizioni**	tairmini/ kondeetseeoni
trade	**commercio**	kommaircho
unique	**unico**	ooneeko
unit	**unità**	ooni-ta
weight	**peso**	payzo
work	**lavoro**	lavoro

SHOPPING

HEARING

Can I help you?	**Posso aiutarla?**	Posso ah-u-taarla?
Would you like anything else?	**Desidera altro?**	Dezeedaira aaltro?
We don't accept this card here.	**Non accettiamo questa carta di credito.**	Non achaytteeamo kwaysta karta dee kraydito.
Can I get you a different size?	**Posso prenderle un'altra taglia?**	Posso prayndairlay oonaaltra ta-lya?

PAYING AND PRICES

Can I use this card here?	**Posso pagare con questa carta?**	Posso pagaray kon kwaysta karta?
Can I pay, please?	**Vorrei pagare, per favore.**	Vo-ray pagaray pair fa-voray.
How much is this?	**Quanto costa?**	Kwanto kosta?

FOOD AND BASICS

Do you have...?	**Avete...?**	Avaytay...?
Can I have...	**Vorrei...**	Vo-ray...
/100 grams.	**/cento grammi.**	/chaynto grammi
/250 grams of ham.	**/duecen-tocinquanta grammi di pro-sciutto.**	/dooay chaynto cheennkwanta grammi dee proshootto.

/0.5 kilos of this cheese.	**/mezzo chilo di questo formaggio.**	/maytso keelo dee kwaysto formajo.
/1 piece.	**/un pezzo.**	/oon paytso.
/2 pieces.	**/due pezzi.**	/dooay paytsee.
/a bit more.	**/un po' di più.**	/oon po dee peew.
/a bit less.	**/un po' di meno.**	/oon po dee mayno.
/0.5 kilo.	**/mezzo chilo.**	/maytso keelo.
/1 kilo.	**/un chilo.**	/oon keelo.
/500 grams of that.	**/cinquecento grammi di quello.**	/cheenkway chaynto grammi dee kwayllo.
/the meat.	**/di carne.**	/dee karnay.
/the sausage.	**/di salsiccia.**	/dee salseecha.
/the cheese.	**/di formaggio.**	/dee formajo.
/the fish.	**/di pesce.**	/dee payshay.
Can I have that piece?	**Potrei avere quel pezzo?**	Potray avairay kwayl paytso?
How much is...?	**Quanto costa...?**	Kwanto kosta?
May I taste a piece of this please?	**Posso assaggiare un pezzo di questo, per favore?**	Posso assajaray oon paytso dee kwaysto pair fa-voray?
Is this sausage/this food spicy?	**Questa salsiccia /questo cibo è piccante?**	Kwaysta salseecha /kwaysto cheebo eh pee-kantay?

Is this sweet?	**È dolce questo?**	Eh dolchay kwaysto?
How long will this keep?	**Quanto tempo si conserva?**	Kwanto taympo see conserva?

USEFUL WORDS

apples	**mele**	maylay
baby food	**cibo per bambini**	cheebo pair bambeeni
baby milk	**latte per bambini**	lattay pair bambeeni
batteries	**batterie**	battaireeay
blue cheese	**formaggio erborinato**	formajo airboreenato
candles	**candele**	kandaylay
coffee	**caffè**	ka-fay
fresh	**fresco**	fraysko
frozen	**surgelato**	soorjaylato
fruit	**frutta**	frootta
gas	**gas**	gaz
joint of meat	**pezzo di carne**	paytso dee karnay
lemon	**limone**	leemonay
matches	**fiammiferi**	feeammeeferi
melons	**meloni**	mayloni

milk (fresh)	**latte (fresco)**	lattay (fraysko)
milk (long life)	**latte (a lunga conservazione)**	lattay (ah loonga konservatseeonay)
mushrooms	**funghi**	foonghee
nappies	**pannolini**	pannoleeni
oil	**olio**	oleo
olives	**olive**	oleevay
onions	**cipolle**	cheepollay
orange	**arance**	aranchay
peaches	**pesche**	payskay
pepper	**pepe (spice)/ peperone (vegetable)**	paypay/ paypay-ronay
salt	**sale**	salay
soap	**sapone**	saponay
stock	**scorta**	scorta
shellfish	**molluschi**	mollooski
tin opener	**apriscatole**	apreeskatolay
toilet paper	**carta igienica**	karta ijenica
toothpaste	**dentifricio**	dentifreecho
washing powder	**detersivo per il bucato**	deterseevo pair eel bookato
washing up liquid	**detersivo per i piatti**	deterseevo pair ee peeattee
water	**acqua**	akwa
wine	**vino**	veeno

SHOPS AND SERVICES

Where is the nearest...?	**Dov'è il più vicino...?**	Doveh eel peew veecheeno...?
Can you repair this?	**Può adjiustarlo?**	Pwo ajoostarlo?
How long will it take?	**Quanto tempo ci vorrà?**	Kwanto taympo chee vor-ra?
I'd like this film developed.	**Vorrei sviluppare questo rullino.**	Vo-ray sveeloo-paray kwaysto roolleeno
How much will it cost?	**Quanto verrà a costare?**	Kwanto ver-ra ah ko-staray?
Can I have this cleaned?	**Vorrei fare lavare questo**	Vo-ray faray la-varay kwaysto

When can I collect it?	**Quando posso ritirarlo?**	Kwando posso riteerarlo

PROBLEMS

This is broken.	**Questo è rotto.**	Kwaysto eh rotto
This doesn't work /doesn't fit.	**Questo non funziona /non va bene.**	Kwaysto non foontseeona /non va baynay
You've charged me too much.	**Mi avete fatto pagare troppo.**	Mee avaytay fatto pa-garay troppo
You haven't given me enough change.	**Non mi ha dato abbastanza resto.**	Non mee ah dato abbastantsa raysto
I'd like a refund.	**Vorrei essere rimborsato.**	Vo-ray ayssairay reemborsaato
I wasn't given a receipt.	**Non mi è stato dato lo scontrino.**	Non mee eh stato dato lo skontreeno
Please can I see the manager.	**Vorrei vedere il direttore.**	Vo-ray vedairay eel deeray-ttoray

USEFUL WORDS – SHOPPING

bakery	**forno**	forno
book shop	**libreria**	leebrair-eea
butcher	**macelleria**	machaylla-reea
camera shop	**negozio di fotografia**	negotseeo dee fotogra-feea
chemist	**farmacia**	farma-cheea
clothes shop	**negozio di abbigliamento**	negotseeo dee abbee-lyamaynto
deli	**rosticceria/ gastronomia**	rosteechay-reea/ gastrono-meea
fishmonger	**pescheria**	payskay-reea
greengrocer	**negozio di frutta e verdura**	negotseeo dee frootta ay verdoo-ra
hardware store	**ferramenta**	ferramaynta
jewellers	**gioielleria**	joeeayllay-reea
map	**pianta della città**	peeanta daylla chee-ta
market	**mercato**	mairkato
music shop	**negozio di dischi**	negotseeo dee deeskee
off-licence	**negozio di alcolici**	negotseeo dee alcolichi
shoe shop	**negozio di calzature**	negotseeo dee kaltsatoo-ray
shoe repair	**calzolaio**	kaaltso-laayo
shop	**negozio**	negotseeo
supermarket	**supermercato**	soopairmairkato
tobacconist	**tabaccaio**	taaba-kkaayo
toy shop	**negozio di giocattoli**	negotseeo dee jokattoli

USEFUL WORDS – SERVICES

car hire	**noleggio auto**	nolayjo owto
dentist	**dentista**	daynteesta
doctor	**medico**	maydico
dry cleaners	**lavaggio a secco**	lavajo ah saykko
garage	**garage/officina**	garajay/ offeecheena
hairdresser	**parrucchiere**	parrookeeairay
police station	**stazione di polizia**	statseeonay dee poli-tseea
post office	**ufficio postale**	ooffeecho postalay
travel agent	**agenzia viaggi**	ajayn-tseea veeajee

CLOTHES AND GIFTS

Where is the main shopping street? — Dov'è la zona più bella per fare shopping? — Doveh la dzona peew bella pair faray shopping?

Is it far from here? — È lontano da qui? — Eh lontano da kwee?

Can I walk? — Posso arrivarci a piedi? — Posso arree-varchee ah peeaydee?

What size is this? — Che taglia è questa? — Kay ta-lya eh kwaysta?

Do you have a smaller size/bigger size? — Avete una taglia più piccola/più grande? — Avaytay oona ta-lya peew peekola/peew graanday?

Where can I try this on? — Dove posso provarlo? — Dovay posso provarlo?

I just want to look around. — Voglio solo dare un'occhiata in giro. — Vo-lyo solo daray oon okkeeata een jeero.

I'm looking for something... — Sto cercando qualcosa... — Sto chairkando kwalkoza...

/more colourful. — /di più colorato. — /dee peew kolorato.

/warmer. — /di più caldo. — /dee peew kaaldo.

/cooler. — /di più fresco. — /dee peew fraysko.

/smart. — /di elegante. — /dee elay-gantay.

/casual. — /di casual. — /dee casual.

Is this in the sale? — Questo è in vendita? — Kwaysto eh een vaynadita?

I'm looking for a present for... — Sto cercando un regalo per... — Sto chairkando oon raygalo pair...

/a child. — /un bambino. — /oon bambeeno.

/a baby. — /un neonato. — /oon nayonato.

/my husband. — /mio marito. — /meeo mareeto.

/my wife. — /mia moglie. — /meea mo-lyay.

/my friend. — /un amico (M)/un'amica (F). — /oon ameeko/oon ameeka.

It doesn't fit me. — Non mi va bene. — Non mee va baynay.

It's perfect. — È perfetto. — Eh pairfaytto.

Can you keep this for me? — Può mettermelo da parte? — Pwo mayttairmelo da partay?

If it doesn't fit, can I bring it back? — Se non mi va bene, posso riportarlo indietro? — Say non mee va baynay posso reeportarlo eendeeaytro?

USEFUL WORDS – CLOTHES AND GIFTS

boutique	**boutique**	boutique
black	**nero**	nairo
blue	**blu**	bloo
bra	**reggiseno**	rayjeesayno
brown	**marrone**	marronay
chequered	**a quadretti**	a kwadrayttee
clothes shop	**negozio di**	negotseeo dee
	abbigliamento	abbeelyamaynto
cotton	**cotone**	kotonay
ear rings	**orecchini**	oraykkeenee
green	**verde**	vairday
hat	**cappello**	kappayllo
jacket	**giacca**	jakka
jewellery	**gioielleria**	joeeayllay-reea
jumper	**maglia**	ma-lya
necklace	**collana**	kollana
orange	**arancio**	arancho
receipt	**scontrino**	skontreeno
red	**rosso**	rosso
shirt	**camicia**	kameecha
socks	**calzini**	kaaltseenee
swimming costume	**costume da bagno**	kostoomay da banyo
stripy	**a righe**	a reegay
tie	**cravatta**	kravatta
top	**top**	top

trousers	**pantaloni**	pantaloni
straps	**bretelle**	braytayllay
underwear	**biancheria**	beeankay-reea
	intima	eentima
watch	**orologio**	orolojo
white	**bianco**	beeanko
wool	**lana**	lana
yellow	**giallo**	jallo

NIGHTLIFE

FINDING OUT WHAT'S ON

What is there to do at night here?	Cosa c'è da fare la sera qui?	Koza chay da faray la saira kwee?
Where can I find out about...	Dove posso trovare informazioni su...	Dovay posso tro-varay eenformatseeoni soo...
/cinemas?	/cinema?	/chee-nayma?
/theatres?	/teatri?	/tayatri?
/the opera?	/l'opera?	/lopera?
/the ballet?	/il balletto?	/eel ballaytto?
/classical music?	/la musica classica?	/la moozika klassika?
Do you have a programme?	Avete un programma?	Avaytay oon programma?
Where can I get a programme?	Dove posso trovare un programma?	Dovay posso tro-varay oon programma?
What's on?	Che cosa danno?	Ke koza daanno?
Who's singing?	Chi canta?	Kee kanta?
When does it start?	Quando comincia?	Kwando komeencha?
When does it end?	Quando finisce?	Kwando fineeshay?
Is there an interval?	C'è un intervallo?	Chay oon eentairvallo?
What language is it in?	In che lingua è?	Een kay leengwa eh?
Have you seen it?	L'ha già visto?	La ja veesto?
Is it good?	È bello?	Eh bayllo?
Can you recommend a film?	Può consigliarmi un film?	Pwo konsee-lyarmee oon film?
Will I be able to follow the story?	Riuscirò a seguire la storia?	Reew-shee-ro ah saygweeray la storia?
Is the film dubbed/subtitled?	Il film è doppiato/ha i sottotitoli?	Eel film eh doppeeato/ah ee sottoteetolee?
Is there anything on in English?	C'è qualcosa in inglese?	Chay kwalkoza een eenglayzay?
Is there somewhere to go for a drink near here?	C'è un posto dove si può bere qualcosa qui vicino?	Chay oon posto dovay see pwo bairay kwalkoza kwee veecheeno?
We're looking for a lively bar.	Stiamo cercando un bar animato.	Steeamo chairkando oon bar aneemato.

We're looking for a quiet bar.	Stiamo cercando un bar tranquillo.	Steeamo chairkando oon bar trankweello
Where are the best bars?	Dove sono i bar migliori?	Dovay sono ee bar mee-lyoree?
Where can we see live music?	Dove possiamo ascoltare musica dal vivo?	Dovay posseeamo askoltaray moozika dal veevo?
Do you know who's on?	Sa chi c'è che suona?	Sa kee chay kay swona?
What sort of music is it?	Che musica fanno?	Kay moozika fanno?
Are they any good?	Sono bravi?	Sono braavi?
🔊 What are the clubs like here?	Come sono i locali notturni qui?	Komay sono ee lokali nottoornee kwee?
🔊 Does it matter what I wear?	È importante come mi vesto?	Eh eemportantay komay mee vaysto?
Is there a good gay club?	Conosce un buon locale gay?	Konoshay oon bwon lokalay gay?
How much does it cost to get in?	Quanto costa entrare?	Kwanto kosta en-traray?

INVITATIONS AND SMALL TALK

🔊 Would you like to have a drink?	Prende qualcosa da bere?	Praynday kwalkoza da bairay?
🔊 Shall we have something to eat?	Mangiamo qualcosa?	Manjamo kwalkoza?
Which clubs do you like?	Quali locali le piacciono?	Kwalee lokali lay peeachono?
I want to go somewhere we can dance.	Vorrei andare in un posto dove si può ballare.	Vo-ray an-daray een oon posto dovay see pwo ba-laray.
🔊 Shall we go there?	Andiamo lì?	Andeeamo lee?
I thought the film was great.	Il film mi è piaciuto moltissimo.	Eel film mee eh peeachooto molteessimo.
I couldn't really follow the film.	Non sono riuscito a seguire veramente il film.	Non sono reewsheeto ah saygweeray vairamayntay eel film.
I really enjoyed the music.	La musica mi è piaciuta veramente.	La moozika mee eh peeachoota vairamayntay.
Have you seen them before?	Li aveva mai visti prima?	Lee avayva my veesti preema?
What do you like to eat?	Cosa vorrebbe mangiare?	Koza vorraybbay man-jaray?

Do you know somewhere good to go round here? **Conosce qualche bel posto dove possiamo andare?** Konoshay kwalkay bayl posto dovay posseeamo an-daray?

ASKING FOR WHAT YOU WANT

Do you have tickets? **Ci sono biglietti?** Chee sono beel-yet-tee?

⚽ Can I have ... tickets for... **Vorrei comprare due biglietti per...** Vo-ray kom-praray dooay beel-yet-tee pair...

/tonight? **/stasera.** /stasaira.
/tomorrow? **/domani.** /daw-mani.
/the matinée? **/lo spettacolo pomeridiano.** /lo spayttakolo pomaireedeeano.

⚽ Could I have seats near the back/the front? **Vorrei dei posti verso il retro della sala/all'inizo della sala?** Vo-ray day po-stee vayrso il raytro daylla saa-la/all'een-it-sio daylla saa-la?

⚽ Can I have...
/an ice cream? **Potrei avere...** Potray avairay...
/popcorn? **/un gelato?** /oon jaylato?
/a drink for the interval? **/dei popcorn?** /day popcorn?
/una bibita per l'intervallo? /oona beebita pair leentairvallo?

USEFUL WORDS

action	**azione**	atseeonay
adventure	**avventura**	avvayntoora
bar	**bar**	bar
casino	**casinò**	casi-no
cinema	**cinema**	chee-nayma
club	**locale**	lokalay
exit	**uscita**	oosheeta
gay club	**locale gay**	lokalay gay
live music	**musica dal vivo**	moozika dal veevo
opera	**opera lirica**	opera leerika
pop	**pop**	pop
rock	**rock**	rock
romance	**storia d'amore**	storia damo-ray
seat	**posto a sedere**	posto ah saydairay
seating plan	**pianta dei posti a sedere**	peeanta day posti ah saydairay
soul	**soul**	soul
subtitled	**sottotitolato**	sottoteetolato
techno	**techno**	techno
ticket	**biglietto**	beel-yet-to
toilets	**bagni**	banyee
traditional	**tradizionale**	tradeetseeo-nalay
tragedy	**tragedia**	trajay-dya

HEALTH

AT THE PHARMACY

Where's the nearest pharmacy?	Dov'è la farmacia più vicina?	Doveh la farma-cheea peew veecheena?
Is there a pharmacy open now?	C'è una farmacia aperta a quest'ora?	Chay oona farma-cheea apairta ah kwaystora?
Is there an all-night pharmacy?	C'è una farmacia aperta tutta la notte?	Chay oona farma-cheea apairta tootta la nottay?
Can I have this prescription, please?	Vorrei queste medicine, per favore.	Vo-ray kwaystay maydee-cheenay pair fa-voray.
Can I take this when I'm pregnant?	Posso prenderle se sono incinta?	Posso prayndairlay say sono eencheenta?
Is there something better I can get on prescription?	Posso avere qualcosa di meglio con la ricetta?	Posso avairay kwalkoza dee may-lyo kon la reechaytta?
I need something for...	Vorrei qualcosa per...	Vo-ray kwalkoza pair...
/a cold.	/il raffreddore.	/eel raffray-doray
/pain.	/il dolore.	/eel do-loray.
/a headache.	/il mal di testa.	/eel mal dee taysta.
/constipation.	/la stitichezza.	/la steeteeketza.
/a cough.	/la tosse.	/la tossay.
/diarrhoea.	/la diarrea.	/la deearraya.
/thrush.	/il mughetto.	/eel moogaytto.
/travel sickness.	/la nausea.	/la now-zay-a.
/tooth ache.	/il mal di denti.	/eel mal dee dayntee.
Can I have...	Vorrei...	Vo-ray...
/some insect repellent?	/un insettifugo.	/oon eensetteefoogo.
/some pain killers?	/un analgesico.	/oon a-nal-jaysiko.
/some cotton wool?	/del cotone idrofilo.	/dayl kotonay eedrofeelo.
/some plasters?	/dei cerotti?	/day chairottee?
/a pregnancy testing kit?	/un kit per il test di gravidanza.	/oon kit pair eel test dee graveedantsa.

HEARING

| Take one/two /three pills | Prenda una/due/ tre pillole. | Praynda oona/dooay/ tray peellolay. |

/one/two/three/four times a day.	/una/due/tre/quattro volte al giorno.	/oona/dooay/tray/kwattro voltay al jorno.
/every... hours.	/ogni... ore.	/onyee... oray.
Take with food.	Lo prenda a stomaco pieno.	Lo praynda ah sto-mako peeayno.

AT THE DOCTOR

Is there a doctor near here?	C'è un dottore qui vicino?	Chay oon dottoray kwee veecheeno?
Is there a doctor I can see now?	C'è un medico che mi possa ricevere subito?	Chay oon may-diko kay mee possa reechay-vairay soobito?
Is there a doctor who speaks English?	C'è un medico che parla inglese?	Chay oon maydiko kay parla eenglayzay?
When is the surgery open?	Quando è aperto l'ambulatorio?	Kwando eh apairto lamboolatoreeo?
Can the doctor come here?	Il dottore può venire qui?	Eel dottoray pwo vayneeray kwee?
It's urgent.	È urgente.	Eh oorjayntay.
Can I see a female doctor?	Posso vedere un medico donna?	Posso vedairay oon maydiko donna?

HEARING

What is the problem?	Che problema c'è?	Kay problayma chay?
How do you feel?	Come si sente?	komay see sayntay?
Where does it hurt?	Dove le fa male?	Dovay lay fa maalay?
How long has it been like that?	Da quanto tempo è così?	Da kwanto taympo eh kozee?
Let me see.	Mi faccia vedere.	Mee facha vedairay.
Please lie down.	Si distenda.	See deestaynda.
It's not serious.	Non è niente di grave.	Non eh neeayn-tay dee gravay.
You need to go to hospital.	Deve andare in ospedale.	Dayvay an-daray een ospay-dalay.
Take this prescription to a pharmacy.	Vada in farmacia con questa ricetta.	Vada een farma-cheea kon kwaysta reechaytta.
Go to a doctor when you get home.	Vada da un medico quando torna a casa.	Vada da oon maydiko kwando torna ah kaza.

YOUR SYMPTOMS

I'm bleeding.	Sto sanguinando.	Sto sangweenando.
I've been vomiting.	Ho vomitato.	Oh vomeetato.
I have a fever.	Ho la febbre.	Oh la faybbray.
Is it serious?	È grave?	Eh gravay?
I'm worried about my...	Sono preoccupato per...	Sono prayokkoopato pair...
/vision.	/la vista.	/la veesta.
/breathing.	/la respirazione.	/la rayspeerat-seeonay.
/heart.	/il cuore.	/eel kworay.
/period.	/il ciclo mestruale.	/eel cheeklo maystrooalay.
It hurts here.	Mi fa male qui.	Mee fa maalay kwee.
I've hurt a muscle in my...	Mi sono stirato un muscolo del...	Mee sono steerato oon mooskolo dayl...
I have a pain in my...	Ho male...	Oh maalay...
/stomach.	/di stomaco.	/dee sto-mako.
/throat.	/di gola.	/dee gola.
/chest.	/al petto.	/al paytto.
/head.	/di testa.	/dee taysta.

/legs.	/alle gambe.	/allay gambay.
/bowels.	/all'intestino.	/alleentaysteeno.
/kidneys.	/ai reni.	/aee raynee.
/ears.	/alle orecchie.	/allay orekkeeay.
It hurts a lot.	Mi fa molto male.	Mee fa molto maalay.
/when I eat.	/quando mangio.	/kwando manjo.
/when I walk.	/quando cammino.	/kwando kammeeno.
/all the time.	/sempre.	/saympray.
/sometimes.	/qualche volta.	/kwalkay volta.
/when I move.	/quando mi muovo.	/kwando mee mwovo.
/when I breathe.	/quando respiro.	/kwando rayspeero.
I have a...	Ho...	oh...
/rash.	/un'irritazione.	/oon eerreetatseeonay.
/lump.	/una protuberanza.	/oona protoobairantsa.
/swelling.	/un gonfiore.	/oon gonfeeoray.

ABOUT YOU ...

I am...	Sono...	Sono...
/diabetic.	/diabetico.	/deeabaytiko.
/pregnant.	/incinta.	/eencheenta.
/on the pill.	Prendo la pillola.	Prayndo la peellola.
I have...	Ho...	Oh...
/asthma.	/l'asma.	/lazma.
/heart problems.	/problemi di cuore.	/problaymee dee kworay.
/high blood pressure.	/la pressione alta.	/la praysseeonay alta.
I feel...	Mi sento...	Mee saynto...
/weak.	/debole.	/daybolay.
/feverish	/la febbre.	/la faybbray.
/hot.	Ho caldo.	Oh kaaldo.
/cold.	/freddo.	/frayddo.
/sick.	/la nausea	/la nousaya.
/dizzy.	/le vertigini.	/le verteegini.

USEFUL WORDS – AT THE DOCTORS

arms	braccia	bracha
back	schiena	skeeayna
birth control	controllo delle nascite	kontrollo dayl-lay nasheetay
bladder	vescica	vaysheeka
bone	osso	osso

burn	bruciatura	broochatoora
chest	petto	paytto
condom	preservativo	praysairvateevo
cream	crema	krayma
cut	taglio	ta-lyo
ears	orecchie	oraykkeeay
eyes	occhi	okkee
fingers	dita	deeta
foot	piede	peeayday
gland	ghiandola	gheeandola
hand	mano	mano
head	testa	taysta
hips	anche	ankay
joint	articolazione	articolatseeonay
knee	ginocchio	jeenokkeeo
legs	gamba	gamba
lump	protuberanza	protoobairantsa
muscles	muscoli	mooskoli
neck	collo	kollo
nose	naso	nazo
pelvis	bacino	bacheeno
pills	pillole	peellolay
rash	irritazione	eerreetatseeonay
shoulder	spalla	spallaa
skin	pelle	payllay

EMERGENCIES

spine	**colonna vertebrale**	kolonna vairtay-bralay
swelling	**gonfiore**	gonfeeoray
teeth	**denti**	dayntee
throat	**gola**	gola
voice	**voce**	vo-chay

EMERGENCIES

Please help me. It's an emergency!	**Mi aiuti, per favore. È un'emergenza!**	Mee ah-u-tee pair fa-voray. Eh oon aymairjayntsa!
You must come quickly.	**Dovete venire subito.**	Dovaytay vayneeray soobito.
I've lost my child.	**Ho perso mio figlio.**	Oh pairso meeo fee-lyo.
Quick!	**Presto!**	Praysto!
Call the police.	**Chiamate la polizia.**	Keeamatay la poli-tseea.
Call an ambulance.	**Chiamate un'ambulanza.**	Keeamatay oonamboolantsa.
Get a doctor.	**Trovate un medico.**	Trovatay oon maydiko.
They're not breathing.	**Non respirano.**	Non rayspee-rano.
They're unconscious.	**Sono svenuti.**	Sono svaynooti.

They're bleeding badly.	**Stanno perdendo molto sangue.**	Stanno pairdendo molto sangway.
They have broken something.	**Si sono rotti qualcosa.**	See sono rotti kwalkoza.
Don't move them!	**Non muoveteli!**	Non mwovay-taylee!
Wait till the ambulance gets here.	**Aspettate che arrivi l'ambulanza.**	Aspay-tatay kay arreevi lamboolantsa.

ATTACK

Help me!	**Aiuto!**	Ah-u-toh!
Please help me, I've been robbed.	**Per favore, mi aiuti, sono stato derubato.**	Pair fa-voray, mee ah-u-tee, sono stato day-roobato.
Please help me, I've been assaulted.	**Per favore, mi aiuti, sono stato aggredito.**	Pair fa-voray, mee ah-u-tee, sono stato aggraydeeto.

LOSS

I'm lost.	Mi sono perso.	Mee sono pairso.
I've lost my child.	Ho perso mio figlio.	Oh pairso meeo fee-lyo.
I've lost my...	Ho perso...	Oh pairso...
/wallet.	/il portafoglio.	/eel portafo-lyo.
/passport.	/il passaporto.	/eel passaporto.
/tickets.	/i biglietti.	/ee beel-yet-tee.
/money.	/i soldi.	/ee soldi.
A few minutes ago.	Alcuni minuti fa.	Alkooni meenooti fa.
One/two hours ago.	Una/due ore fa.	Oona/dooay oray fa.
Yesterday.	Ieri.	Eeairee.

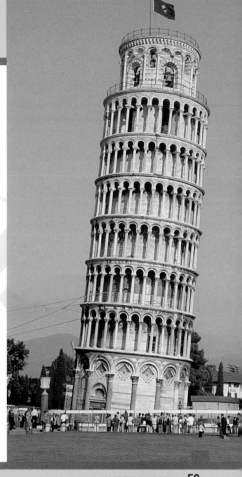

ROME – CITY ESSENTIALS

Rome is a frenetic, traffic-ridden and yet beautiful city of around 3.5 million people. The streets come alive every summer as people throng the pavement cafés and bars and take early evening promenades through the squares and piazzas.

It is justly famed for the huge number of ancient and cultural sites it has to offer. The Vatican on its own is a state, with churches, museums and sights that are some of the world's greatest. Just over the River Tiber are the ruins and legacy of ancient and Christian Rome. It's no wonder so many people make wishes to return at the Fontana di Trevi.

WHEN TO GO
Rome's warm climate makes a visit at any time of year pleasant except, perhaps, if you don't like hot weather, in which case avoid July and August.

Rome is always busy, and there's no quiet season. Easter is especially hectic, as are many of the other festivals on the Christian calendar, but it's worth visiting at the same time just to join in. An opera season lasts from December to June, and an increasing number of other events means there's always something going on.

TOURIST OFFICES
The main tourist offices are on the Via Nazionale near the Palazzo delle Esposizioni, at Stazione Termini at Imperial Fora and Largo Corrado Ricci.

GETTING AROUND

Many of Rome's ancient sites are clustered within walking distance of each other – and getting around on foot is easy. You'll also find that much of the central city is closed to traffic, so you should expect to do some walking. Travel by car is difficult, so only do it if you have to.

METRO

The Metro is the quickest way to get around Rome. Tickets are inexpensive and you can buy them from tobacconists, newspaper kiosks or at vending machines at the stations themselves. If you intend to do a lot of travelling, buy a daily or weekly pass, which will also give you unlimited bus travel.

Metro stations are marked with a big red 'M'. There are two main lines. Line A runs from Anagnina to Battistini in the north. Line B runs from Laurentina to Rebibbia. Change lines at Termini.

BUS AND TRAM

Buses and trams can be slow, but do go to most parts of Rome. Stops are marked Fermata – and a yellow sign will tell you which buses and destinations the stop serves. Most journeys will cost only a standard flat-rate fare – but you must have a ticket before you get on, and get it stamped by the machine. You can buy tickets at tobacconists, newspaper kiosks and at bus terminals.

TAXI

Taxi prices can be high, so be prepared to pay for convenience. In theory, there are taxi stands – or you can hail your own taxi on the street – but, in practice, you'll find it easier to get your hotel or waiter to phone for one for you.

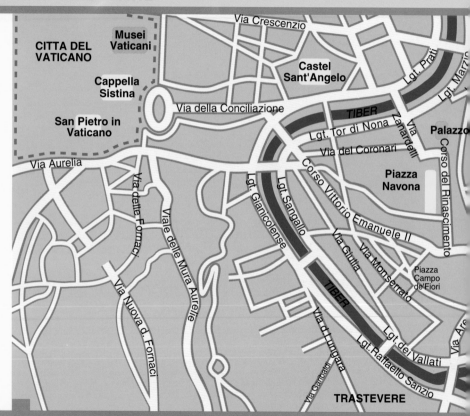

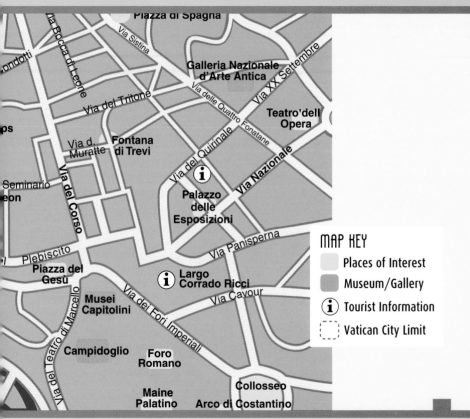

Piazza di Spagna

Via Sistina

Galleria Nazionale
d'Arte Antica

Via delle Quattro Fonatane

Via XX Settembre

Via del Tritone

Teatro'dell
Opera

ps

Via d.
Muratte

Fontana
di Trevi

Via del Quirinale

Via Nazionale

Seminario
eon

Via del Corso

(i)

Palazzo
delle
Esposizioni

Plebiscito

Via Panisperna

Piazza del
Gesù

(i) Largo
Corrado Ricci

Via Cavour

Musei
Capitolini

Via dei Fori Imperiali

Via del Teatro di Marcello

Campidoglio

Foro
Romano

Maine
Palatino

Collosseo

Arco di Costantino

MAP KEY

- Places of Interest
- Museum/Gallery
- (i) Tourist Information
- Vatican City Limit

THINGS TO SEE AND DO

SHOPPING

For refinement – and sometimes sheer expense – Rome's shopping is remarkable. But you don't have to be rich to find good clothes and shoes, as there are always bargains to be had. For clothes, the Via dei Condotti and surrounding streets, such as Via Bocca di Leone, have a classy reputation. For younger, and less expensive, fashion try the streets around Piazza di Spagna and also Via del Corso. For antiques, the main areas are on Via del Babuino and Via del Monserrato, but only if you have some money to spend – or just like looking. For shoes – that Italian and Roman speciality – try Via dei Condotti or Via Nazionale.

MARKETS

Campo de' Fiori is an open air food market, open mornings, Monday to Saturday. On this site heretics were occasionally burned at the stake. It's worth a walk even if you're not out to shop. The Piazza Vittorio Emanuele is a food, fish and meat market. Also try the indoor produce market at Piazza Alessandria, open mornings till noon, Monday to Saturday. For something visually stunning try Via Trionfale – a colourful flower market.

For shoes and seconds try Bancarelle di Scarpe a Testaccio, on Piazza Testaccio, every day except Sunday.

If junk and bargains are your thing, join the Romans and other tourists at Porto Portese, a busy Sunday morning junk market that's been running since World War II. If you want an early start, it begins at dawn! Also try the Saturday junk market on Via Sannio by the church of San Giovanni in Laterano.

WITH CHILDREN

Ice cream might be a good place to start, since most children will take it as seriously as the Italians do. If you want to give them the real thing go to a gelateria. Rome's ancient sites also offer some exciting experiences for children – the claustrophobic and crowded climb up the Dome of St Peter's Basilica, and the view when you get there, for example. Another idea is a trip to the catacombs of St Sebastian, and also of St Callixtus, where early Christians buried their dead. The passages are dark and you often have to join a tour, but the paintings and feel of the tombs are worth it.

AFTER DARK

For an evening meal, take a wander through Trastevere across the river from the ancient city. Most areas have pizzerias and restaurants where you can eat good Italian food at reasonable prices. Nightlife for many

Italians means sitting long into the warm summer evenings and talking with friends outside a café or pizzeria. For music – especially Latin dance – try Via di Monte Testaccio.

LOCAL SPECIALITIES

A proper meal begins with an antipasto (hors d'oeuvre). Roman specialities include salads with anchovy and garlic, cippolle agro-dolce (sweet and sour onions) and grilled or baked aubergine, called melanzane.

Next is the primo piatto, or first course, which will be soup, pasta or rice. Pasta is chosen to match the accompanying sauce – tubes of cannelloni are filled with a meat or spinach sauce, gnocchi alla romana is an oven-baked dish with cheese and butter, and ravioli are pasta squares filled with meat or cheese. Then comes the primi, or main course. Typical dishes are baccala (salt cod), and abbacchio (young lamb).

With the food must go wine – and Italy is one of the world's largest producers, so there is plenty of good wine from nearby regions to choose from.

MUSEUMS AND GALLERIES

The Vatican, to the west of Rome across the Tiber, holds many of the city's greatest treasures. There are over ten museums, and you can see Michelangelo's Sistine Chapel and frescoes by Raphael. Of the museums, the Museo Gregoriano-Etrusco is wonderful for the aesthetic beauty of its objects, while the Pinocoteca gallery has works by Giotto and Raphael. For sculpture, go to the Museo Pio-Clementino and Museo Gregoriano Profano.

In Rome itself, the Galleria Borghese, on Via Borghese, is the biggest of the city's galleries and has works by Bernini, Caravaggio and Raphael. The world's oldest public museums, the Musei Capitolini (Capitoline Museums), are unmissable. The famous 'She-wolf' statue can be found in the Palazzo dei Conservatori; while the sculpture of Marcus Aurelius stands in the Palazzo Nuovo.

Further north is the Galleria Nazionale d'Arte Antica in the Palazzo Barberini, off the Via delle Quattro Fontane, dedicated to art of the 13th–16th centuries. The Museo Nazionale Estrusco, meanwhile, in the Villa Giulia on Via delle Belle Arti, holds a huge collection of Estruscan artefacts. For Greek and Roman antiquities Museo Nazionale Romano at the Palazzo Massimo alle Terme, Piazza del Cinquecento, and the Palazzo Altemps, Piazza di Sant`Apollinare, holds an unmissable collection.

Unless you have information to the contrary, assume that museums are closed in afternoons and on Mondays.

ENJOYING ROME

There are enough ancient sites, buildings and ruins in and around, Rome to fill months of visiting and you're sure to discover your own favourite places. The Colosseum – ancient Rome's place of entertainment and gory spectacle – is perhaps one of the world's most stunning monuments, and even though you may have seen it hundreds of times in photographs, seeing it for real will still be a memorable experience.

The present state of the Colosseum is largely due to the pillaging of stone during the 15th century for, among other buildings, San Pietro in Vaticano (St Peter's Basilica). Near to the Colosseum is the Arco di Costantino (Arch of Constantine) on Piazza del Colosseo.

West of the Colosseum lies the great Foro Romano (Roman Forum), or public places of ancient Rome. This mass of ruined temples and buildings spans more than a thousand years of history. Here you will find the ruins of the Templo di Vesta, or Temple of the Vestal Virgins, and the Colonna Traiana, a beautifully sculptured column celebrating ancient Rome's victories over the Dacians – who lived in what is now Romania. You'll also find the Palatino here – the residential hill of ancient Rome's elite, now mostly hidden under the gardens of Orti Farnesiani.

Further towards the Tiber is the elegant and impressive Campidoglio (Capitoline Hill), the administrative centre of ancient Rome, designed by Michelangelo in the 1530s. Approach from the stepped avenue of la Cordonata for the best visual impact.

One of ancient Rome's best preserved and most impressive buildings is the Pantheon, Piazza della Rotonda. Built by Hadrian in 128 AD the Pantheon remained the largest free-standing dome in the world until the 1960s. It became a Christian church in 609 AD. From here, it's a block or so to the Chiesa del Gesù (church of Gesù), at Plaza del Gesú. If it looks familiar that's because it's been imitated all over Europe. If you head west from the Pantheon you'll find the Piazza Navona, a place of unspoiled baroque beauty, great for people watching. Northeast of the Chiesa del Gesù is the Fontana di Trevi, in the Piazza of the same name.

To the north are the famous Spanish Steps, or the Piazza di Spagna, a favourite meeting place and a perfect spot to rest. You can climb the steps for a splendid view of Rome. Nearby, north up the Via del Babuino, is the church of Santa Maria del Popolo and the Piazza del Popolo. The church contains beautiful frescoes, and works by Caravaggio.

To the south of the Colosseum is the Terme di Caracalla, the best preserved of Rome's great public baths. Nearby is the Via Appia Antica (Appian Way), built in 312 BC, and lined by tombs and catacombs.

However you choose to fill your time in Rome, and whatever your purpose in going, the magic of this city is sure to draw you back again and again, with a new discovery waiting for you around every corner.